THE PROVERBIAL *Woman*

Being a Wise Woman in a Wild World

Robin Chaddock

WINEPRESS **WP** PUBLISHING

2nd printing January, 2001.

Printed in the United States of America

Packaged by WinePress Publishing, PO Box 428, Enumclaw, WA 98022. The views expressed or implied in this work do not necessarily reflect those of WinePress Publishing. Ultimate design, content, and editorial accuracy of this work is the responsibility of the author.

Unless otherwise noted all scriptures are taken from NIV, New International Version, Copyright © 1973, 1978, 1984 by the International Bible Society. Used by permission of Zondervan Publishing House. The "NIV" and "New International Version" trademarks are registered in the United States Patent and Trademark Office by International Bible Society.

Verses marked NASB are taken from the New American Standard Bible, © 1960, 1963, 1968, 1971, 1972, 1973, 1975, 1977 by The Lockman Foundation. Used by permission.

Verses marked TEV are taken from The Bible in Today's English (Good News Bible), © American Bible Society 1966, 1971, 1976. Used by permission.

ISBN 1-57921-267-0
Library of Congress Catalog Card Number: 00-100228

Dedication

Lovingly dedicated to Almighty God who allowed me this voice in the conversation, and to my beloved husband, David, who allowed me the time and space to do the speaking.

Acknowledgments

My heartfelt thanks to

my tremendous husband for the gift of belief in me

two remarkable children who ate a lot of frozen food

my Email cheerleading group for constantly praying me through this project

the staff of Second Presbyterian Church for their perpetual encouragement and interest

Uncle George, Pam Hatfield and Ken Stanley for their trust

Winepress for making a dream a reality

God's Holy Spirit for walking with me and guiding my path every step of the way

Table of Contents

Foreword

I am absolutely terrible with directions. These days, to be politically correct, I guess you would call someone like me "directionally challenged." I have come to the point in my life where, if I actually arrive at my desired location, I feel so very, very blessed. Because of this "glitch" in my character, I have become a regular at gas stations, asking anyone who looks friendly for verbal aid to my destination.

I remember being excited one day about visiting a new fabric and craft superstore that had opened in a large town about 35 minutes from my home. I got to the town like a champion, but soon found myself leaving that town behind without finding my new superstore. So, off to a gas station I drove to begin my familiar search for a person with a kind face. I asked a large man at pump number one if he knew the way to the fabulous new fabric store. He said, in a very disinterested voice, that he thought it was off such-and-such road, next to McDonald's or something. I don't think he was a fabric kind of guy. I decided to try someone else, perhaps someone with less testosterone. I found two ladies giggling on their way into a restaurant. When I asked them for some guidance they said, "Oh yeah, that is such a great store!" One went on to say that she too had a hard time finding it. I am sure she was only trying to make me feel better, but then she gave me basic, practical directions that made the voyage seem very simple indeed. She told me stores and landmarks to look for, as well as tricky places in the road. When I left I was even more excited about finding my way to that fabric monstrosity. Following my kind guide's instructions, I eventually got to the store; it was worth the struggle, believe me.

Every time I encounter the "Proverbial Woman," I immediately feel as if I am faced with a very long journey. This woman's character seems so foreign to me, and yet *so* very desirable. I want to follow her example and live every area of my life with such intentional discipline and beauty. However, the trip between the cluttered place I stand and the golden ground her feet grace, seems somewhat exhausting. Where do I begin?

There is, of course, never a more perfect map than scripture, but I often find it an added blessing when a seasoned traveler takes his or her finger and traces along the seemingly tangled lines, making clear the path we are called to walk. When you listen to someone who has walked it ahead of you, you get to embrace the wisdom that can only come from experience. That is the kind of counsel I found in this wonderful book.

When I first read this book, I was struck time and again by the way Robin shares from her heart the different lessons the Lord taught her. As she takes her finger and traces a clear definition of what it means to be a "wise woman in a wild world," I was thankful that she seems genuinely concerned with my journey (not like the man at pump number one). Like those giggling ladies, Robin gives us clear direction we can use and renews our excitement for our destination.

Robin's honesty is so fresh and comforting as she shares with her readers that the journey to becoming a woman of beauty and substance, like the proverbial gal, is not only a struggle for us at times, but that she, too, has struggled along this selfless path. She gives us "warning areas" that might need construction along the way, such as pride, wrong attitudes, undisciplined lips, unyielding hearts. As I passed through the pages of this book, I started to feel the effects of Robin's contagious passion to become the woman God designed her to be. I realized that if I want to experience *all* Christ has for me, I must, through His strength, "press on toward the goal to win the prize for which God has called me heavenward in Christ Jesus" (Phil. 3:14 NIV).

Do you know what? I am excited! I am excited about this book. I am excited about all that Robin has learned and now shares. I am excited about my own journey with Christ. I am excited about the changes we could all witness in our hearts, our families, our communities, and our world if we would set out for the journey so clearly "mapped-out," which will lead us to a treasure in our character. Just think, all this great direction and we won't even have to stop at a gas station. Thanks, Robin. Thank you, Lord!

Melissa Jansen
Author, *Are You Kidding, God! Me, a Prudent Woman?*

Introduction

Congratulations! The mere fact that you picked up this book makes you a Proverbial Woman in Training, or, as my witty friend Debbie puts it, a P-WIT. You have answered a tug to pursue wisdom in our wild world.

We live in a wild world where the magazine covers at the check-out stand give false images of desirable womanhood. We live in a realm where families are fractured and personal lives are shattered by the power of gold and the media-fied view of success and normal life. We live in a crazy society that has made day into night, and night into day—and no one really knows what the hour is.

In the midst of the relativism, the false gods, the chaos of choice, and the murkiness of morality, the book of Proverbs comes crashing through like a breath of fresh air. Short, sweet, and full of "Do this and live, do this and die," it stands as a port in the storm. Lady Wisdom extends her hand to the sinking and the searching. Her words are so simple, they seem unreal.

As for the original Proverbial Woman, well, it's time to make peace with her. If we're intimidated by her, it's more about us than about her. The startling truth is that the Proverbial Woman—the woman in Proverbs 31—is you! As you read this book, remember that this famous/infamous chapter is about characteristics and attitudes, not credentials and accomplishments. You have the same qualities she has, you just have to uncover the unique ways they manifest in you as you grow in the love of God and the power of the Holy Spirit.

The original Proverbial Woman was obviously married with children. A modern Proverbial Woman holds any and many stations in life. You may be married, single, or divorced. You may be a single-mother, a career woman, or a domestic administrator. It doesn't matter if you have a family living in the same home with you, or if your family is the family of faith at church. You may live at work, you may live alone, or you may live in a house full of people. Wisdom knows no age boundary, no economic structure, no family configuration, and no occupational limit. Wisdom is for everyone.

Read this book with a friend or a group. There are nearly as many questions as statements in these pages. They are not rhetorical, for the most part. The questions are posed to assist your discovery of all you have in common with our sister, this Hebraic wife, businesswoman, artisan and mother.

God bless you as you open yourself up to the pursuit of wisdom and the transformation it will bring to your work, your self-image, your relationships, and the depth to which you know and experience God.

CHAPTER ONE

The Proverbial Party

proverb (n.) – a short, popular saying expressing an obvious truth *(Webster's New World Dictionary)*.

It was an invitation I couldn't refuse. We were sitting on the porch of our favorite restaurant on a balmy Pasadena New Year's Eve. Under the twinkling Italian lights, the man I had been crazy in love with for over a year invited me to spend the rest of my life with him.

A year and a month earlier, he had called to extend an invitation for our first date. We both loved jazz, and he asked if I would accompany him to a New Year's Eve Jazz Party. I had to decline because I had already accepted an invitation from another gentleman, but I wanted to kick myself for not being available! With that first date proposition, I knew my interest was being returned, and I cut the other fellow loose shortly after New Year's Day.

What made the invitation on the patio so charming was the way my dear fiancé started the question. "A year ago, I asked you to join me for New Year's Eve and you had already accepted another invitation. Tonight, I want to make sure that never happens again."

The Invitation

You are loved. You are deeply loved, passionately loved, and eternally loved. The One who loves you is Almighty, the Maker of Heaven and Earth. He came to earth in flesh to prove to you His love. You are never out of His sight, His care, His grace, nor His ability.

He is the same God who sent His good friend and constant companion, Wisdom (Prov. 8:22, 23), to issue an invitation that is hand-addressed, scented, and delivered with care in a beautiful envelope. God loves you so much that He made the way plain to living life fully, enthusiastically, and honestly. He makes the invitation to His party so clear and exciting that you will never accept anyone else's inferior, or imitation, invitation again. He loves you and desires your company that much. Many times I have heard a woman say, "I just wish God would write something on the wall or in the sky so I can understand the way to go." Cheer up, dear sister. Becoming a Proverbial Woman will set you on the unchanging trail of understanding that promises a level path and firm footing (Prov. 4:26).

Let's take a look at the invitation, the hostess, and the benefits of attending this Proverbial Party.

When you send out an invitation, you prepare for your guests. Dame Wisdom is no exception. Proverbs 9:1–6 tells us:

Wisdom has built her house, she has hewn seven pillars; She has prepared her food, she has mixed her wine; She has also set her table. She has sent out her maidens, she calls from the tops of the heights of the city: "Whoever is naive, let him turn in here!" To him who lacks understanding she says, "Come, eat of my food and drink the wine I have mixed. Forsake your folly and live, and proceed in the way of understanding." (NAS)

When you accept Wisdom's invitation, you start on the path of the Proverbial Woman. As a woman of wisdom, you accept an invitation to change your life in three critical ways. The party favors include, but are not limited to, peace, purpose, and passion.

Peace. You accept the invitation to consider peace. We all have to admit it at one time or another. We are carrying around a somatic illness, a physical outgrowth of a spiritual/emotional ailment that we could perhaps be freed from if we let peace rule our lives. I carry my stress in my neck and shoulders. They are my early and immediate warning system that something is not right in my life. The muscles in those body parts let me know when there is something internal or external that I need to examine, something with which I need to make peace. When you are a Proverbial Woman, you live your life with honesty and integrity. That is good for your peace of mind and soul.

Purpose. You accept the invitation to live your life on purpose. Becoming a woman of wisdom means you have learned to strip away the temptations and expectations of the world, you have learned what is truly important, you know who you are, and you live each and every day accordingly. You realize for whom and for what you have been created. This changes your life.

I had an experience in my late 30's in which I was invited to a weekend retreat called "The Great Banquet." Those who had attended raved about the experience. I, being a bit skeptical and suspicious by nature, dragged my feet at going. "It will change your life," they raved. I liked my life just the way it was. Well, not really, but one weekend away, doing things I had always done before at church retreats, was not going to make that much difference.

But I went. After all, it was a weekend away, and it would get those people to stop bugging me about going.

The first night, my suspicions were confirmed. There was a presentation given on priorities. I went to my sleeping bag saying, "OK, OK, God. I know I focus too much on my job, but that's only because You haven't blessed us with enough money to get out of debt. I have to work like a dog to keep us afloat. I know I'm a short-tempered Mommy, but with all the work I have to do, I don't have time to pay attention to my kids. I know my marriage isn't a priority right now, but we'll work on that later—after we get out of debt and the kids are out of the house. Well, all right, I'll get my priorities back in line. I'll put my family first and try to be a better person." With that, I went to sleep. I was confident that with my two seminary degrees, Christian upbringing, time spent as a church employee, and basic love for God, I wouldn't have to make any other resolutions for the weekend. I was done, and could now smugly sit by and watch everyone else get their houses in order.

I could never have suspected what was going to happen the next morning. After breakfast, we were invited to walk quietly into the small chapel at our church. There on the communion table was the most captivating, mesmerizing portrait of Christ I had ever seen. His gaze was fixed right on me. His mouth turned up slightly in invitation to come closer, and in pleasure that I had already come so far. His beautiful brown eyes brimmed with love for me. For me. As clearly as if the picture had audibly spoken the words, He gently corrected nearly forty years of faulty focus, saying, "It's not about you, Robin. It's about me. It's not about your priorities and getting everything all straightened out. It's not about you engineering every task and every day to get ahead. It's about me loving you, and you living day by day, minute by minute, in that deep, passionate, eternal love."

I was speechless, and my focus has never been the same.

Power. The third point of the invitation seems antithetical to the one just before it, but they really do fit together. The third strand is the invitation to assume the power to take control of your life. As a Proverbial Woman, a woman of wisdom, you will be in control of your days, your choices, your tongue, and your responses.

The invitation has been sent. Now why should you come to the party?

Why Pursue Wisdom?

I live in the Midwest. Snow and sleet are not strangers to any of us here. That does not, however, mean we like or feel comfortable with them.

One Thursday in February, after speaking at my alma mater to a group of college women about their forever identity as God's daughters, I hopped into my van and started the hour-long trek home. A light rain started to fall.

As I traveled south on the main freeway to my home, the light rain quickly turned to heavy rain, then to slushy snow accompanied by gusting winds. It had also gotten dark. I soon realized that my hands and the steering wheel had become fused together as I struggled to keep my van on the road—especially when semitrailers came rushing by, pelting my van with muck, ice and slop. I was scared.

As each truck swooshed by, I thought, "I have just had a wonderful time delivering a very important message in a place that is so meaningful to me, and now it's the last thing I'll ever do. I'll never see my sweet husband or my two wonderful children again." (Near death brings out the drama in all of us!) Then my eyes locked on my salvation.

I discovered what many people already know. Or maybe, at the moment it made so much sense to me, that I saw it again for the first time. The white line by the side of the road shone as the lifeline by which I could keep my bearings and know I was going to be all right. I kept that guide in sight. My hands relaxed, my shoulders dropped, and I made it home in one wet, cold, sloppy piece.

Wisdom is our guide, our escort, our helmsman through the stormy, muck-slinging days, as well as our advisor and companion through the fair weather times. Wisdom is as obvious and available as the white line by the side of the road; as constant as that painted beacon that keeps us all from careening down the bumpy, treacherous roads.

Proverbs 3:13–18 and 21–26 sum up the many benefits of answering positively to wisdom's invitation:

Blessed is the one who finds wisdom, the one who gains understanding, for she is more profitable than silver and yields better returns than gold. She is more precious than rubies; nothing you can desire can compare with her. Long life is in her right hand; in her left hand are riches and honor. Her ways are pleasant ways, and all her paths are peace. She is a tree of life to those who embrace her; those who lay hold of her will be blessed. My child, preserve sound judgment and discernment, do not let them out of your sight; they will be life for you, an ornament to grace your neck. Then you will go on your way in safety, and your foot will not stumble; when you lie down, you will not be afraid; when you lie down, your sleep will be sweet. Have no fear of sudden disaster or of the ruin that overtakes the wicked, for the Lord will be your confidence and will keep your foot from being snared.

That's a pretty tall order. There is a long list of benefits, or excellent returns, when you invest your life in the pursuit of wisdom. Let's look at several of these advantages in everyday woman terms.

Happiness. Happiness is another term for blessedness. How many people around us every day are chasing how many things, trying to find happiness? How many possessions, provisions, and prizes are we pursuing on a perpetual basis, looking for that moment when we feel we can exhale and relax because we have finally made it? Happiness is readily available to those who pursue wisdom because we are told that "the fear of the Lord is the beginning of wisdom" (Prov. 9:10). Fear is reverence, respect, and honor. Fear of the Lord means we are struck with awe by His being, power, capabilities, and character. Fear of the Lord draws us into a mysterious intimacy with the Almighty that effectively blocks out our ability to be obsessed with ourselves, our schemes, and our solutions to our problems. Happiness is being saved from ourselves when we have a full-fledged ambition to seek God's face and embrace His dear friend Wisdom in the process.

Riches, Honor, and Length of Days. Riches and honor are listed in Wisdom's treasure chest, as is a long life. When looking at those benefits, we must always be aware that God's ways are not our ways, and His thoughts not our thoughts (Isa. 55:8). While God may indeed bless us with the same riches, honor, and long life that we imagine from a human perspective, one of the true benefits of pursuing and grasping Wisdom is the transformation in our thinking and values that comes from putting God's ways first—honoring God.

For roughly thirty-nine years of my life, I could think of nothing more desirable than a comfortable home, a modest closet full of clothes, a nice car to drive, understated elegance in jewelry, and the smug (and fake) humility of being a recognizable and noteworthy person. I did everything I could to make all of this happen. My favorite thing to do was work. My passion was career advancement. More work, more money. Better career, better earning power. Even after my children were born, work was the focal driving point of my life.

All the while, I was becoming more miserable. Caring for the kids kept me from putting all of my energy and ambition into earning money. Domestic responsibilities hindered me from pursuing riches and honor as I had defined them. No job could make me money fast enough. On top of all that, we were going into debt at such a rate that we had to give up our big, custom-built home for a smaller house. As blinded as I was by the god Jesus called Mammon, I did not even realize that "We eventually cannot afford what we most desire—deep relationships. For if 'time is money' and people take time, then the 'opportunity costs of relationships (the gain that we would earn by doing something else) will be prohibitive and intimate friendships will be few. 'Spending' time with friends is costly; we could 'invest' it better elsewhere."[1]

I am grateful every day for God's grace and mercy. He allowed me to come to the end of myself, to grow up, and to come to maturity in Him day after day, which helped me see the beauty and riches in my life as it was. Thankfully, He didn't have to bring me any tragedies to jolt me into submission. In His persistence and goodness, He introduced me to His friend Wisdom and suggested I get to know her intimately and permanently.

Because of Wisdom's friendship, I have discovered that kids are not a condiment in life, something you throw on top of everything else when it is convenient. To smell your child's hair, to hear him giggle, to break up a fight, and to speak words of instruction every day—only to hear them repeated to a younger sibling at a later time—are some of the richest experiences available. To smile at your beloved spouse across the room and know that there is deep affection between you, to share openly and honestly with your life's partner on a regular basis, and to have him speak kind words of you in public, are honors saved only for those who are patient, watchful, and wise. Long life is measured by the laughter around a simple meal with good friends. Length of days is assessed by the evenings you can lay your head on your pillow knowing that your very life has meant something to someone else that day. Those are the riches and honor of wisdom. That is the length of days that reverence for God will put into your life.

Peace and Pleasantness. One of our deepest longings is for peace of mind. So why are we constantly trading pleasant ways for selfish ways, harmony for haughtiness, orderliness for orneriness, and tranquillity for truckloads of stuff? Wisdom promises peace and pleasantness. Maybe this lacks the excitement and danger that our adrenaline-addicted society demands on a daily basis to stay stimulated and alive. The difference between the two life-styles, however, is the contrast between being constantly buzzed and then abandoned by caffeine, and being cleansed and renewed by fresh spring water. The first one seems to be the way to being fully alive, but only provides diminishing returns as a person is catapulted down the spiral of addiction and increasing need.

Perhaps the most tangible and necessary way wisdom provides peace is through a good night's sleep (Prov. 3:24). As Proverbial Women, we sleep better because our integrity, honesty, love—and the rewards of that love—will move us through our days and into nights that have no regrets.

How many times have you gone to bed saying, "I wish I hadn't said that today"? How many times have you been awakened with a start in the middle of the night thinking, "Oh, how am I going to solve this problem?" How many times have you risen early, but felt there wasn't any particular reason to get out of bed?

As we learn from Wisdom how to speak, act, and respond as a woman of wisdom, we will lay our head on the pillow at night able to rest securely in God's arms. We will sleep soundly and awake refreshed in the morning, ready to move out into the new day with purpose and peace, taking the Master's hand for the next adventure.

No Fear. What are you afraid of? Financial hardship? A child straying? Not being important or recognized? Getting to the end of life and wondering what happened?

Not having enough? An affair? Wisdom promises that when we walk in step with her, we will have nothing to fear. That does not mean we may not fall on hard times. Her promise is that we will not have cause to fear. Being a Proverbial Woman means we know who we are in God's world and in God's heart. It means we tend our relationships to make them strong and healthy. Being a woman of wisdom means we each understand our mission and live that mission with passion. It means we have life's priorities in proper order. It also means we are so in tune with the needs in ourselves and in others—and the resources to meet those needs—that we have no time for idle fretting!

Sure Feet. One summer, during the four years I was Director of Youth Ministries at my church, I took the kids to a Young Life camp in Colorado. Young Life camps are not for the fainthearted. Every day is packed with a new adventure.

One day, it was my cabin's turn to take on the challenge of the ropes course. A ropes course is a series of logs, bridges, and swings a fair number of feet off the ground. Although each person is on a belay line—which saves you from hurting the ground should you lose your footing—it is still a frightening experience for many.

I was one of the many. The first test of the ropes course was to walk one-foot-in-front-of-the-other up a log that angled from the ground to a spot on another tree about twenty feet up, where the actual course began. From there, I had to walk across another 20-foot log until I reached the "safety" of the next task, the rope bridge. Being a counselor, I had to do this. Staying securely on the ground was not an option for one in leadership!

My knees shook. I clenched the belay line with my hands, as if it would do me some good in steadying my trembling body. I wanted to cry, but could show no fear. My mind was screaming out, "Don't do this to us! Have you no sense?"

I made it up the inclined log and then across the suspended log. It took a long time, but I did it. Every step was accompanied by the sure conviction that my wobbly legs were going to give out, and I was going to get hurt. But by the grace of God, I made it.

What makes you go weak in the knees? Walking into a room full of strangers—or friends? Heights? Balancing the checkbook? Thinking about facing one more day of dirty diapers or endless paperwork? Confrontation with your family? The thought of tending a dying child or parent?

Wisdom promises us that our feet, our steps, our path will be steady and secure as we become better friends with this gift of God (Prov. 3:26). Because reverence for the Lord is the beginning of wisdom, our sights are taken off our feet and set on the author and finisher of our faith (Heb. 12:2). Our eyes are taken off the raging seas around us and fixed on the hand and face of the one who controls everything (Mark 4:35–41).

The Original Proverbial Woman

She has been hated; she has been dismissed. She has been the source of finger- wagging by men and chagrin among women at whom those fingers were wagged. She is the woman described by King Lemuel's mother in the thirty-first chapter of the book of Proverbs. When I first met her, I did not know whether to kick her or kiss her. Should I bless her because she gives some wonderful guidelines, or should I curse her because she sets an impossible standard? As Melissa Jansen says, "When I see all the areas in which this woman displays prudent living, I realize I have two choices. The first is to cut Proverbs 31 out of my husband's Bible so he doesn't get any ideas. The second is to be challenged enough to change."[2]

Well, the wise thing to do when you do not know much about certain people—before you decide to write them off—is to get to know them at least a little. After all, we are to do to others what we want them to do to us (Matt. 7:12).

So I started snooping around to see what this woman is all about. Thankfully, there are at least three ideas about this superheroine that make it a bit more possible to be in the same room with her.

Composite. Perhaps the king's mother had taken a survey of the best qualities available in Hebrew women at the time. As she penned her advise to her son (imagine being her daughter-in-law), she drew on all the superlatives she could find. The Proverbial Woman may be a composite, much as if we took pictures of individual women doing the most noteworthy things a woman can do and pasted them all together.

Poetry. The first letter of each line in this acrostic poem is the successive letter of the Hebraic alphabet. This woman has so many wonderful features because there were twenty-two letters in the alphabet! If we were to write the same poem today, our charged-up woman would have twenty-six remarkable characteristics.

Lifetime Overview. Annie Chapman suggests "Proverbs 31 is a list of lifetime accomplishment, rather than a log of a particular day. When I look at Proverbs 31 as a life-time resume of a mature woman, it gives me hope."[3] This view suggests that this litany of notable qualities is a description of a woman who is past middle age, and who has had a long time to accomplish many things and develop many skills. It might be the kind of speech given at a retirement dinner or at a sixtieth birthday banquet.

Any of these views give hope to the young, the harried, and the vexed! Our Proverbial friend is a woman just like us, who has grasped the one ingredient necessary to make her a distinguished woman and an example for the rest of us: "A woman who fears the Lord, she is to be praised" (Prov. 31:30b).

When we look at her and growl, it reminds me of my dog Maggie looking at her reflection in a mirror while she plays with a chew toy. Maggie does not know she is actually looking at herself. She thinks there is another dog trying to take something precious away from her. Maggie's defensiveness comes from the fact that she is focused on herself and fears that she is going to lose something in a struggle.

When we roll our eyes, groan, or make that disdainful sniffing sound at the mention of this woman, we are doing so because we have our eyes on ourselves and are growling at our own reflection.

If you are intimidated or disgusted by this woman, if you are tempted to throw her example out with the bath water, reexamine what you focus on in creation. You may be glued to the creature and not the Creator. Instead of dismissing this important passage of scripture because you feel you cannot measure up, embrace this passage as a picture of the possibilities—and more—when you seek God's face and Wisdom's friendship.

The most important thing to remember is this: she was not honored by God because she was a superwoman. She was a super woman because she honored God.

How Do You Become a Proverbial Woman?

If you want all of the benefits discussed in this chapter so far, plus many more, you want to become a Proverbial Woman, a woman of wisdom. This woman has six distinguishing features that color her life with satisfaction, abundance, peace, and honor. The rest of this book will unpack these traits, show you how to make them your own, and give real-life examples of women who have been changed for God's glory as they decided to walk hand-in-hand with an eternal and trusted friend, Wisdom.

You are a Proverbial Woman, a woman of wisdom, when you let God:

1. Draw you to Himself. The end of the quest is also the beginning. "The fear of the Lord is the beginning of Wisdom" (Prov. 9:10). We will lay the foundation for becoming a woman of wisdom. How do we get started? What do we need to do in actual step-by-step instructions to get into the proper relationship with God that allows wisdom to infiltrate and transform our lives?

2. Work through you. We will look at the zeal you will gain for life when you grasp and understand the mission for which you have been created. Your days and years will be energized as you learn to say no to the temptations that cloud your understanding of the essence of God's call on your life. Your vision will gain clarity and your behavior will

resemble more a steady stream than a raging rapid. The Proverbial Woman was very sure of her call and capabilities. She lived her life with noticeable passion and effectiveness.

3. Communicate through you. For anyone who has ever said, "I should have said . . ." or "I wish I hadn't said . . .", we will look at the top ten ways you can be a woman of wise speech. If you have ever bemoaned, "I should have listened when . . .", we will explore how to discern the wise advisor from the fool. We will unpack passages in Proverbs which give us unmistakable advice for speaking and listening.

4. Minister through you. As far as she was able, The Proverbial Woman "extended her hand to the poor and the needy" (Prov. 31:20). She not only ministered directly to those in obvious need, she acted as a support to those closest to her, enabling them to carry on their missions in the community. Her service flowed naturally in all she did and all she was.

5. Laugh through you. The Proverbial Woman was a terrific steward. She took care of herself, her family, and her community. She watched over all God had given her. Because she was so faithful, she made an impact wherever she went and she could "laugh at the days to come" (Prov. 31:25). This laughter signaled a light heart as she entered each day knowing all was well. She looked ahead, invested wisely, cared for the details, and could hum her way through life, confident that the cold

winds could blow and she and those she loved would be protected.

6. Love through you. Whatever your family configuration, you are part of a birth family and a global family. We will look at three ways in particular to be the gift to others that God created you to be.

Your RSVP

If you are like most of the women I have surveyed, the first envelopes you open when you shuffle through the daily mail are the envelopes that have been hand-addressed, have a return address from someone you know and love, perhaps have been scented, and are packaged in a beautiful paper that sets them apart from the rest.

The invitation has been sent. You have opened the envelope. You may now choose to throw the invitation on the pile of unheeded and unanswered mail, but the invitation has been extended just the same.

If you choose not to respond positively, please examine your reason. Is it akin to the excuses given by the guests specially invited to the Great Banquet in Luke 14:15–24? Are you too busy to pursue wisdom? Are you afraid you won't know anyone at the party? Are you just not interested in having your life transformed into the beauty God intended for you? Do you simply prefer to design your own parties for one?

I responded to the invitation of my soon-to-be husband under those sparkling lights with a resounding, "Yes!" There was no hesitation, no deliberation. I certainly could not foresee everything the future would hold for us, but I knew he was the one I wanted to go with into that future.

I said yes to the invitation, and I've been saying yes to the marriage every day since.

I encourage you to RSVP positively to this Proverbial Party. Follow through on your budding desire to become a Proverbial Woman, and walk through the door to the most exciting life-long event you'll ever attend!

Your Proverbial Action Step

The book of Proverbs has thirty-one chapters. Most months have thirty-one days. For three months read the chapter which corresponds to the date. Select a proverb each day which stands out to you. In a small notebook or journal, write that proverb. Ask the Holy Spirit to seal it in your heart. Make any notes on the changes in your life.

CHAPTER TWO

The Bottom Line

The Proverbial Connection – *Charm is deceptive, and beauty is fleeting; but a woman who fears the Lord is to be praised. Give her the reward she has earned, and let her works bring her praise at the city gate* (Proverbs 31:30–31).

Accepting the invitation and stepping into the party begs the very first question, How do I get started? Yes, I want to have more peace and purpose in my life! Yes, I want to speak, act, think and relate more wisely. Yes, I want to walk hand-in-hand with Wisdom and her creator, God Almighty. But how do I do it?

Our quest is outlined by one very short half-verse in our guidebook, the book of Proverbs: "The fear of the Lord is the beginning of wisdom" (Prov. 9:10). This fear is one of awe, of appreciating the mighty distinction between God and me, and God in me. Through the gift of the Holy Spirit, God dwells in me. Because I am created in God's image, God shines through me. But I must never forget that I am creature, not Creator. I am beloved, not the Lover. God is present in all that I see, but all that I see does not sum total God. There is much more. We can meditate, study, pray, discuss, and ponder God our whole lives and only scratch the surface of His being. Through His presence in our joys and anguish, we have a veiled sense of the immeasurable depth of God's love, wisdom and might. "But no full understanding is possible; only a holy fear, a trembling in the face of the immeasurable."[1]

To more fully appreciate the assertion that properly relating to God is the beginning of wisdom, we must look at the contrast between two highly prominent women in the Old Testament. Both had very similar characteristics and ambitions. The stark difference is found in their foundation, the tilt of their heart.

One name in the Old Testament is synonymous with evil, treachery, greed, and vanity. Fear reigns in the heart today when a woman is nicknamed Jezebel! The book of 2 Kings tells of her devotion to her husband's career. After all, as long as Ahab was king, Jezebel was, of course, queen. She possessed incredible people management skills, evidenced by the huge stable of Baal prophets she directed. She ran a huge household, serving as many as 850 people at dinner in one sitting. She was skilled in land acquisition. She was beautiful, smart, and had well-defined goals. She shared many qualities with the Proverbial Woman outlined in Proverbs 31:10–31.

But Jezebel lacked one critical leaning. She did not honor or revere the Lord. She killed God's prophets and slandered his kings. She put her stock in her looks, her husband's position, the massive entourage she had cultivated, and her ability to make people do exactly what she wanted.

Just before her demise, reported in 2 Kings 9:30–37, she "painted her eyes and arranged her hair." She taunted Jehu, God's appointed king, as he came for a visit. She yelled at him from an upper story window and he replied by instructing two or three men inside to push her through. The telling of her death is rather gruesome in the details, but one aspect is quite noteworthy. After Jehu had eaten a meal and taken drink, he directed Jezebel be buried, for, after all, "she was a king's daughter" (v.34). When the people who were to bury her went outside to gather her body, "they found nothing except her skull, her feet, and her hands" (v.35). There was nothing left of the woman! Because of her evil, the Lord ordained that she could not be found by anyone, forever after. "This is the word of the Lord that he spoke through his servant Elijah the Tishbite: On the plot of ground at Jezreel dogs will devour Jezebel's flesh. Jezebel's body will be like refuse on the ground in the plot at Jezreel, so that no one will be able to say, 'This is Jezebel'" (vv. 36–37). After all of her conquests, commands, cosmetics, and career moves, there was not a thing left of her life. Because of her faulty grounding, her life and legacy meant absolutely nothing.

"Charm is deceptive and beauty is fleeting, but a woman who fears the Lord is to be praised" (Prov. 31:30). This Proverbial Woman had her focus set on pleasing God. She put aside worldly ambitions and expectations. She decided not to believe the fashion magazines and the gossip shows. She kept her sights on the One who made her, loved her and intimately guided the steps of her day. Because of this, her legacy lived on, her name was exalted in the city gates, and her family spoke of her for years to come. Her life meant something. Her work was carried on. Her hands are also noted in this famous passage. She extended them to the poor and the needy (v. 20), and worked willingly using her gifts and talents to provide for the community and her family (vv. 13, 19).

Graciously, the book of Proverbs gives us deeper insight into the pursuit and capture of wisdom in our lives. In two well-defined steps, God and His companion Wisdom show us how to live in honor, reverence, awe, and fear of the Lord. In one beautiful poetic couplet, we are given the keys to tranquillity, passion, and influence.

In the world of business and finance, the bottom line refers to the summary of a cost-benefit analysis. After business owners have weighed what they will need to invest, expend, or sacrifice over against the probable gains, they look at the bottom line and decide if this will be worth the time, energy, and capital of their company. Proverbs 3:5–6 calls us to the bottom line. If you want to become a woman of wisdom, here is the charge and the promise—the bottom line.

Trust in the Lord with all of your heart and lean not on your own understanding. In all your ways acknowledge him, and he will make your paths straight (Prov. 3:5–6).

Trust in the Lord. What is trust? Trust is sitting down in a chair, flipping on a light switch, or entering into the stoplight intersection when you have the green light . Dr. William G. Enright, Senior Minister of Second Presbyterian Church in Indianapolis says, "Trust is a combination of competence and reliability." With this definition of trust, we can be certain our faith in God is well-grounded.

God's competence is God's might. God's competence is centered in God's wisdom and design. Is God able to handle the situation? Is the creator of the universe and the God who deeply, passionately, and eternally loves you, capable of understanding and directing your life? Do you truly believe what the angel Gabriel said to Mary, that "nothing is impossible with God" (Luke 1:37)? God asks Job many questions about God's competence as Job comes to a more genuine understanding of God in his life. After Job has been tested, not only by Satan, but by his well-meaning friends, God takes over the conversation. He brings Job to a higher level of awareness and awe of the Almighty's work and wonder in the universe and in Job's life.

> *Have you given orders to the morning, or shown the dawn to its place? Have you journeyed to the springs of the sea, or walked in the recesses of the deep? Do you know the laws of the heavens? Can you set up God's dominion over the earth? Can you raise your voice to the clouds, and cover yourself with a flood of water?* (Job 38:12,16,33–34)

The answer to these and many more questions is, of course, a sheepishly resounding "No." But God does not intend to humiliate Job, or us, with these questions. He intends to lovingly and accurately turn our perspective so we can again know that He is in control, that He has set everything in motion, and that He is able to guide our lives with passion and precision. God does not seek to indict, but to invite, as He bids us look at the mind- and heart-expanding wonders of His competence.

By wisdom the Lord laid the earth's foundations,
By understanding he set the heavens in place;
By his knowledge the deeps were divided,
And the clouds let drop the dew (Prov. 3:19–20).

God's reliability is God's faithfulness. Moses comforts the people of Israel during a leadership transition when he encourages and promises, "Be strong and courageous. Do not be afraid or terrified because of them, for the Lord your God goes with you; he will never leave you nor forsake you" (Deut. 31:6). Does God have a good track record in Scripture and in the everyday lives of contemporary people of faith? Psalm 139:7–10 asks,

> *Where can I go from your Spirit? Where can I flee from your presence? If I go up to the heavens, you are there; if I make my bed in the depths, you are there. If I rise on the wings of the dawn, if I settle on the far side of the sea, even there your hand will guide me, your right hand will hold me fast.*

Have you ever known God to drop the ball? As Cheri Fuller says, "When I would take a baby step toward God by praying about something, He'd answer and I'd see a little more of His faithfulness. It was as if He was saying, 'Yes, I'm here. I care. I'm faithful. Keep coming to me'— much as we stretch out our hands to our little ones when they take their first steps."[2]

Why are we afraid to trust God? We cannot help humanizing God. Especially when we are young in faith, we think God is like the other authority figures in our lives. If we have trouble trusting God, it may reflect a neglectful father, an overprotective mother, an abusive older sibling, or an unpredictable grandparent. Over time, with good nurture and modeling from steady people of faith, those uncertainties and blocks can be overcome. We must often trust God's word, choosing to set aside the conditioning of our past lives. To move into a deeper place of trust, we need to constantly pray for the transforming work of the Holy Spirit, and then watch for the transformation as it unfolds. In short, we need to remember that God is not those who have hurt us in the past, and those who have hurt us in the past were not acting as representatives of God.

But what if God intends to take us someplace we don't want to go? When I was a newly blossoming teenager, a missionary couple came to speak at the Sunday evening service at my church. I have no clear memory of what they said, but I have a very clear memory of being scared to death that I was going to have to do what they had done. If I was going to be a real disciple, I would have to go to heinous and scary places to prove my love for God. But this view of faith completely omits God's great love for me, His deep and passionate love that seeks communion with me. It totally eliminates the understanding that God created me for a purpose, and that my joy would be complete in the fulfilling of that purpose. "The place God calls you to is the place where your deep gladness and the world's deep hunger meet."[3]

But what if trusting God means I have to give up control? Well, the good news/bad news is that that is exactly what it means! This objection simply shows an absence of understanding and faith in Scripture and in the nature of God's competence and reliability. It divorces us from God and denies the truth that God has been and continues to be at work for our benefit to give us a future and a hope (Jer. 29:11). The God who loves you deeply, passionately, and eternally is your partner, not your puppet master. What do you want to control that you think you can handle better than God can? What do you want to keep from His view and direction? And why is it in your life anyway if you want to keep it from God?

Lastly, every day the newscast and the morning paper give us new examples of children who have been abused by someone they love and trust. Increasingly the statistics rise, and we know of more and more children who suffer this indignant injustice. One of the most heartbreaking consequences is their inability to form intimate relationships with others, especially God. The abuse may even have been religious, what one therapist calls "spiritual rape," in which the child had religious truths forced upon him or her without regard to conversation, questions, or individual temperament. The struggle is then enormous to come to comfort in God's presence, in the silence, and in the warmth of God's care. One may be able to lead a religious life, but true trust and delight in being a child of God, a partner with God, and a lover of God, is absent. The difference between knowing about God and knowing God is monumental.

All of these reasons why it is difficult to trust God are worthy of critical and thorough examination. They are real and powerful roadblocks to the many rich returns of wisdom we uncovered in chapter one. Do not let them take you prisoner any longer. Realize that it is now time to heal and to take charge of your response to these spiritual obstacles. The power to come to a deeper trust in God is in the dynamic alliance of you and the Holy Spirit.

Lean not on your own understanding. What is understanding? Look in a thesaurus and it's easy to see the wisdom in giving God control of your heart, vision, and direction. What is our intelligence compared to God's? What is our grasp on the overall big picture of our lives relative to God's view of our lives? How does our awareness of world and historical events stack up to the overall discernment

God has? When we take a good look at these questions and their answers, it becomes almost comical that any of us should lean on our own understanding. It would be funny, except that it is often so tragic.

This is the final responsibility we have in our part of the bottom line *In all your ways acknowledge Him* (Prov. 3:6). Pray with your life, not just your head. Make it a practice in the morning and in the evening to bookend your day with prayer. In the morning look for guidance; in the evening express your gratitude. Orient yourself to be set up in constant communication with the Holy Spirit and in communion with God.

"In all your ways" has at least four connotations:

1. Manner. In the way you are, acknowledge God. In your speech, your dress, and your attitudes, let on to others that God is the authority of your life. When we say, "She just has a certain manner about her," let that manner or spirit about you declare the presence of the Holy Spirit in your life.

2. Means. How do you get things done? In what way do you operate? Do you approach life and situations with hope, honesty, and respect for others? Do you work with integrity? Are you demanding, cooperative, passive, forceful, commanding, inviting? The way you get things done—the means to your ends—needs to confirm your relationship with God. You acknowledge or disavow God in your life as you move through your daily chores and conversations. Do others see you acknowledge God in your ways?

3. Miles. Where are you going? In your relationships, your finances, your career, and your acquisitions,

do you acknowledge or recognize God? Do you see and appreciate God? Do you reply and respond to God in openness and gratitude? To acknowledge God in our miles means we are aware of the decisions we need to make, and we turn to God for direction. We listen for the still, small voice that says, "This is the way. Walk in it" (Isa. 30:21).

4. Milieu. Does your environment tell others that God is walking by your side? Would others know by looking at the magazines on your coffee table, the art on your walls, and the trappings of your surroundings that you are in a loving, peace-filled relationship with the Almighty? Are you living in chaos or order? (I didn't say perfect cleanliness!) Does your atmosphere reflect peace or agitation?

When you acknowledge God in these ways, you open the doors for His guidance. You and God partner to let people know who you are and whose you are. The Holy Spirit can then more smoothly and effortlessly flow through and over you to guide and direct your steps, your interactions, and your reflections so that you are walking in wisdom.

How do we acknowledge God?

P–Pause. Stop for a moment and look at the sky, or drink in the scents and sounds of your favorite season. Savor the taste of your "comfort food." Take time to really hug a friend, hold a child, or kiss your beloved. Our five senses are the first five gifts God gave us upon birth. He is constantly showering us with messages of His desire for us to enjoy His world and all the gifts therein. When you honestly take in a truly pleasurable sensory experience, your soul will often sigh, "aah." That sigh is a prayer of gratitude and an acknowledgment of God's grace and cleverness in creation.

R–Reflect. One of the best ways to reflect is in writing. Anne Broyles ponders, "We are gifted with a space and time to open ourselves to the Lover of the World. Journaling is a private discipline in which we can reveal ourselves totally. There is no need to carefully consider words or wonder what other people might think of our thoughts. Journal writing is sharing between our true selves and the God of Truth. In journaling, we come to know ourselves as we really are and feel the acceptance of the One who loves us no matter what."[4]

Journal writing can provide the following benefits:

- bring perspective to emotions safely and effectively,

- promote meditation and prayer time,

- give an overview to the day's activities and evening's thankfulness,

- bring a release from stress and anxiety,

- unfold new insights and deeper understanding of God's word.

You don't need to aspire to be a writer, just a pursuer of wisdom. Keep a notebook with you at all times; you never know when you will have the opportunity to commune with and acknowledge God in this way. One day, I got a flat tire on the freeway. After I walked to the nearest gas station to call my husband for help, I had the chance to journal the experience while I waited for the white steed to arrive with my knight astride!

A–Ask. Microsoft has an advertising campaign that asks, "Where do you want to go today?" Technology has the ability to so expand our world that in a few keystrokes on the computer, you can access almost anything in the world. One morning as I was gazing at the picture of Christ I often use for meditation, I found myself looking into His eyes and saying, "Where do you want me to go today?" We acknowledge God when we put ourselves wholly at His disposal—to walk where He needs us to walk, say what He needs us to say, and do what He needs us to do. The result is often a contented heart at the end of the day. You lay your head to rest saying, "Boy, today turned out to be a lot different that I thought it might, but I sure feel good about what happened."

Y–Yack. God enjoys a good chat just as much as the next, uh, person. He says, "Call to me and I will answer you," (Jer. 33:3) and "Come now, let us reason together" (Isa. 1:18). My good friend Karen calls me several times a week because she always seems to have something to share. Her daughter is an excellent gymnast, her home-based business is going very well, and she often has amusing and earthy insights to pass along. When she calls, we just chat. We catch each other up on the little happenings of the day, be they happy or challenging. Over the years, these little chats have helped forge quite a friendship. Without them, we would lose touch and would not know the quirky little nuances that keep us honest about ourselves and our day-to-day interactions.

In the moments when you simply acknowledge that God is with you, when you realize that He already knows what you're thinking (so you may as well openly share and discuss it), your relationship with Him deepens and it becomes increasingly easy to walk hand-in-hand with Him guiding your steps. Just chat with Him on a regular and natural basis.

It all adds up to PRAY. Prayer is how we live our lives with God. Do we split God off from our senses, our talents, our goals and dreams, and our routine communications? Or can we, with gratitude and relief, rest with the psalmist who says,

> O Lord, you have searched me and you know me. You know when I sit and when I rise; you perceive my thoughts from afar. You discern my going out and my lying down; you are familiar with all my ways. Before a word is on my tongue you know it completely, O Lord. You hem me in—behind and before; you have laid your hand upon me. Such knowledge is too wonderful for me, too lofty for me to attain (Ps. 139:1–6).

The more we acknowledge God, the more known and understood we feel. The more we invite the Almighty into everything we do and are, the more assured we are of His unconditional acceptance, provision, and love for us.

The cost, then, is to trust, to prefer the vision of the One who sees and knows everything, and to daily ask, "Where would you have me go today?"

The benefit, or the promise, is so simple it is often overlooked or disregarded. **And he will make your paths straight**. So bland on the surface, but so radical when embraced with expectancy, integrity, and gusto!

That means we can lay anything before the Lord and can count on Him to guide our path. Are the finances a puzzle? Are you at the end of your rope with your children, your neighbor, or your spouse? What is the next career or ministry step for you? Should you say "yes" to being on that committee, or being chairman of that board? How should you best share the joy you are feeling over a significant rite of passage? Should you stay in that house or find something else? What should you do with that catastrophic loss? What is the next step in that significant relationship?

The directions God gives are clear. They surface and resurface above all of the "chatter" in your head. Some directions will be compelling and will need to be acted on obediently, in short order, such as Jonah's call to Ninevah. Other directions will unfold over time, as was the path of Joseph from despised brother to dear benefactor. Remember, as God is unfolding things for you, He's directing and leading the paths of thousands of others. The orchestration may take some earthly time to come to fruition.

Some directions will make your heart sing! You will be relieved and astounded to see the hand of God sweeping through your situation. When I received the confirmation that it was time to start Proverbial Women Ministries, I felt incredible liberation and glee. Since the time of that call, a number of people have commented on the change in my demeanor. Peacefulness has come over me, filling my very soul.

Some directions will break your heart for that season in time. Those times in particular, you will want to rely heavily on the promise that, as you are obedient, God is competent and reliable to lovingly and wisely direct your life.

You may have experienced what I lived through in college. When one attends a Christian college and is just shy of twenty years old, one automatically assumes that

everything that happens on campus is thoroughly ordained by God to be exactly the way it appears for the
balance of time, no questions asked. That includes falling
head over heels in love with an absolutely wonderful man.

As the relationship unfolded, however, it became pain-
fully apparent that our future lives were going to take us
in very separate directions. But how could this be? I would
sit in our chapel on campus in absolute agony and pray,
"God, why did you so powerfully bring us together? Why
did you let me fall so hopelessly in love with him if he's
not the one I'm supposed to marry?" God still gave me
the choice, and since God rules and overrules, He would
have made the best out of what I chose. However, I still
knew in my heart of hearts that it was not going to be in
the best interests of either of us to enter into the sacred
and beautiful covenant of marriage. The path certainly
seemed cruel to me.

I had to give God time for the fuller path to be revealed. Your path in question may include a career change,
a child who falls terminally ill, or a friend who turns out
to be something other than what you anticipated. God
only expects that we trust, give way to His insight, and
call on Him daily for the next minute. As Lord Chesterton
of England indicated, when we care for the minutes, the
hours take care of themselves.[5]

In which direction does your heart lean? Are you
Jezebel, with plans, designs, and dreams that don't include
God, or have you turned your heart, soul, mind, and
strength over to the gracious, perfect, and exciting direction of God? Chances are very good that you are some-
where in the middle. My prayer for you is this: as you read,

reflect on, and apply the rest of this book, you will be moved to decide more and more for God each day.

Your Proverbial Action Step

Prayerfully and thoughtfully consider Fredrick Buechner's quote on page 39, "The place God calls you to is the place where your deep gladness and the world's deep hunger meet." What do you perceive to be your deep gladness? What do you believe to be a deep hunger in this world? Ask the Holy Spirit to sharpen and enable you to know and act on your call.

CHAPTER THREE

Your Industrial Revolution

The Proverbial Connection – *She selects wool and flax, and works with eager hands. She is like the merchant ships, bringing her food from afar. She gets up while it is still dark; she provides food for her family and portions for her servant girls. She sets about her work vigorously; her arms are strong for her tasks* (Prov. 31:13–15, 17).

It happens at least once a month. I receive a flyer in the mail promising that, if I attend a certain seminar or all-day workshop, I will become a better manager of time, projects, and people. The brochure assures me that I will become masterful at getting more accomplished in a day; I will have the ability to tackle multiple tasks; and I will be more productive in the number of items I can check off my to-do list.

It wasn't until I had taken a course or two like this that I realized the ironic truth: I don't want to do more in my day! I want to do less. What I want more of is a sense of meaning and cohesion in what I do. I want to live my life on purpose, not just run about checking things off a list, lengthening my resume, or playing super mom.

Do less? Was I nuts? I'll never get anywhere in this life if I do less. My children will be undereducated, understimulated, and generally unfit to enter the college of our choice. My house will be a wreck, and my nails will be a sight. People won't recognize me at the store for all the benevolent work I've done in the community or the advances I've made in my career. What was I thinking?

But I was suffering from a disease called choice-itis. There were too many choices in my life, and they were all so tempting. ". . . choice is no longer a state of mind. Choice has become a value, a priority, a right. To be modern is to be addicted to choice and change. These are the unquestioned essence of modern life. In the modern world there are simply too many choices, too many people to relate to, too much to do, too much to see, too much to read, too much to catch up with and follow, too much to buy."[1] With each new choice we feel more drawn to something better, something bigger, something that will make our life richer or easier. Soon we are chasing every option that comes our way with no sense of who we truly are in the first place. We are those in James who are tossed about by every wave of alternative, only to find ourselves breathless and disoriented as we are smashed on the shore (James 1:6).

Your Industrial Revolution is about doing less in your life, not more. If you are weary of management specialists who don't know you, or your situation and personality, take heart. The greatest Management Specialist of them all knows your design and your path intimately. If you are tired of "too much," the way of wisdom will clarify, simplify, and affirm your deep longing to live at peace with who the Almighty fashioned you to be. Let's look at the Proverbial Woman on letting God work through us. We will explore doing less in a day, but doing it with more passion, purpose, and power than ever before. Our days will become more satisfying; our lives will become more congruent.

What is the word our society uses for people who are perceived to be inert, unproductive, or not achieving to the highest potential? We call those people lazy. But many of us feel unproductive or unfulfilled—even when we run from the time our feet hit the floor in the morning, to the time we collapse into bed at night. Women, especially, are flying through the days at a breakneck pace to carry out volunteer commitments, get the kids where they need to be, manage and meet work deadlines and obligations, keep everyone and everything in the house reasonably clean, and maybe squeeze in some exercise or quiet on a sporadic basis. I know very few lazy women.

I do know a fair number who are really busy, but are also burned out, despondent, unfocused, and mission-less. Some are downright depressed as they look at the unfolding day and think, "Am I just going to do yesterday all over again?" They lack direction, design, and determination because they are lacking the control and order that wisdom brings to life.

Busyness is really a symptom of a deeper uneasiness. Busyness often has two root causes: general anxiety and fear of what others are going to say about us.

We are unable to be still when we are highly anxious. Today, a woman's general anxiety may focus on everything from shootings at grade schools to how the food budget is going to stretch for the week. It can encompass wondering if the right man will ever be available, to wondering if the one coming home will be civil to her and to the children. We look at what others have, do, and are, and we mostly come up short. To fill the gaps, we stay busy.

A specific and prevalent anxiety is the fear of what others are going to say about us. How do our careers stack up? Our decisions? Our children, spouse, house, volunteer commitments, clothing, financial situation, faith walk, social circles, and on and on and on. We run ourselves ragged in the relentless pursuit of as much as, if not more than, the Joneses. We see it all the time. One neighbor signs little Agnes up for cheerleading camp and next thing you know, all the little girls in the neighborhood are signed up for cheerleading camp. Sheila at work has moved into a very comfortable new condo complex. Suddenly everyone is checking into the rates at that complex. Sarah, in the Monday morning Bible Study, has signed up to help in the hospital guild, and a week later the whole group has volunteered to help in the hospital guild—especially if it's *the place* to be for seeing and being seen.

Externally motivated women are very busy women. They do not appear lazy.

The lengths to which we will go to keep up pretenses are remarkable. In 1980, the movie "Ordinary People" starred Academy Award-nominated Mary Tyler Moore as a mother who had lost her beloved older son to a boating accident. The strain of the loss wore on her, her husband, and their surviving son, who believed he had caused the death. Her son went through extensive therapy. Her husband handled his grief as authentically as he could. She stayed busy, unable to forgive her younger son and move successfully through her grief. To keep her overwhelming anxiety at bay, she insulated herself with possessions and suburban activities. In the end, as father and son became more real, she chose to leave the family, not wanting to let down the facade of pristine perfection, the veneer of invulnerability. We trade activity for truth, appearances for integrity, accolades for the souls of our families and our very selves.

But action is not the opposite of laziness— true laziness—as described in Proverbs. Laziness is not the opposite of frenetic activity. Laziness is the opposite of focus.

Throughout Proverbs, a wonderfully descriptive word is used for the lazy and idle. It is *sluggard.* The root word obviously being "slug." As portrayed in Proverbs, this person is so pathetic that when he puts his hand in the food dish, he won't even raise it back up to his mouth (Prov. 19:24). Sluggards are so afraid of working that they make up wild excuses like, "There is a lion outside. I will be murdered in the streets" to avoid going out (22:13).

In modern terms, the sluggard is one who is not willing to do the hard work of life. "The sluggard does not plow in season; so at harvest time he looks but finds nothing" (Prov. 20:4). We can run about scattering seeds, sprinkling water, digging up lots of dirt, and thinking there will be a harvest. But if the timing, intention, or motivation for the work is off, there will be no harvest. While there is lots of activity, there is no real hard work. The woman of wisdom knows the difference.

The hard work of life takes us back to The Bottom Line of the first chapter and the wonderful instruction, "Trust in the Lord with all of your heart and lean not on your own understanding. In all your ways acknowledge Him and He will make your paths straight" (Prov. 3:5–6).

The true hard work of life boils down to three things:

1. Put aside what others think (Trust in the Lord),

2. Say "no" to temptations (Lean not on your own understanding),

3. Concentrate on what God calls *you* to do (Acknowledge Him).

The opposite of being a sluggard is being a woman who walks in step with the Master, who knows who she is and whose she is, who lives a life of centered intentionality and peace, and who moves through her days with a sense of divine mission. In a world filled with choices, knowing and following your path will keep you from becoming overwhelmed, buried, defeated, and despondent. That is the loving design of a very wise God.

Many people who participate in The Proverbial Woman retreat or workshop resonate with the difference between "busy" and "active." Being busy holds the image of flitting and hurrying to accomplish a list of tasks. Being active has a more controlled, focussed feel to it. We can be busy with lots of activities and chores. We can also be actively involved in projects and missions of our choosing as we understand our call and our path. Are you "busy", spinning out of control, or are you "active", engaged in an ordered flow that springs from a sense of purpose?

Perhaps the most striking biblical account of someone living with focus and purpose stemming from a clearly defined mission, is Jesus' meeting with Satan in the desert. This encounter is documented in three of the four gospels, most extensively in Matthew.

Then Jesus was lead by the Spirit into the desert to be tempted by the devil. After fasting forty days and forty nights, he was hungry. The tempter came to him and said, "If you are the Son of God, tell these stones to become bread." Jesus answered, "It is written: 'Man does not live on bread alone, but on every word that comes from the mouth of God.'" Then the devil took him to the holy city and had him stand on the highest point of the temple. "If you are the Son of God," he said, "throw yourself down. For it is written: 'He will command his angels concerning you, and they will lift you up in their hands, so that you will not strike your foot against a stone.'" Jesus answered him, "It is also written: 'Do not put the Lord your God to the test.'" Again, the devil took him to a very high mountain and showed him all the kingdoms of the world and their splendor. "All this I will give you," he said, "if you bow down and worship me." Jesus said to him, "Away from me, Satan! For it is written: 'Worship the Lord your God, and serve him only.'" Then the devil left him, and the angels came and attended him (Matt. 4:1–11).

Provision, protection, possessions. Satan knows how to hit us right where we are vulnerable. Satan knows there are many slick little ways he can tempt us to give up our God-given identity and purpose. The Master Deceiver knows how to mask huge sinkholes with lush, green grass and beautiful wildflowers. Let's look at each trap for what it really is.

Provision. The Tempter knew precisely where Jesus was vulnerable. Jesus had been fasting forty days. For many of us, forty minutes without some kind of snack is a stretch. Jesus was hungry, very hungry, so Satan offered Him the opportunity to eat. Satan extended the invitation to satisfy a need, a worthy need, in exchange for His understanding of His higher call.

There are many needs. We need security, food, shelter, clothing, affection, and a sense of being valued and appreciated. Satisfying needs is not in itself evil. The means by which we satisfy our needs can be.

Satan tempted Jesus to change the nature of things in order to satisfy His needs. The world changes the nature of wants to needs, then invites us to change ourselves and the things around us to meet those "needs".

We are invited to change ourselves from the Temple of the Holy Spirit to a sexual object to meet needs for affection, acceptance, and love.

We are encouraged to change our children into recreated images of ourselves to satisfy our needs for approval, validation, and immortality. We exchange their childhood for an endless string of activities and stimulation to "prepare them for their future."

We are enticed to take a higher paying job that does not match our call, our mission, or our interests to make more money because we need a better home, food, clothing, or social outlet.

What God created to be one thing, we change to something else because we cannot, or will not, wait for or accept His provision.

Jesus knew that he must not change those stones, must not alter their God-given essence. He let Satan know that He would not compromise Himself nor God's creation to miss out on the higher banquet awaiting Him in God's word.

Protection. At first blush, this temptation appears to be Satan's urge to Jesus to save Himself from bodily harm. Satan is encouraging Jesus to put aside what He already knows about God's care for Him, to test it one more time. Let's just see if God will protect you one more time; after all, you are God's Son.

A closer look reveals that Satan is calling on Jesus to protect His name, to defend His reputation, to cement His place in the world. Jesus is solicited to prove what He already knows about Himself and His loving, heavenly Father. Satan wants Jesus to be lured into a competition, a childish game of "prove it."

Anytime you sense a dare, a gauntlet being thrown on the ground, a temptation to do something because it will prove who you are, run—do not walk—away! These games of "prove it" often start with phrases like, "If you're a Christian . . .", or "If you were a good employee, wife, mother, member of the community, woman, friend . . ."

Anytime you are asked to trade your understanding of your God-given mission, your leaning on God's instruction for your life, or the steps God has directed to protect your name, reputation, or public standing, you can be assured you are being enticed to trade your call for something inferior.

Possessions. This one seems rather obvious. After all, anyone with their head on straight and their feet firmly planted in Proverbs 3:5–6 could see this one coming a mile off. Because Satan knows it is "useless to spread a net in full view of the birds" (Prov. 1:17), he asks us to trade our essence for possessions in very subtle ways.

Satan urged Christ to simply bow down, just this once, to worship him. This small investment would net him all the kingdoms of the world and their splendor. Seems a small price to pay for a twenty-five second act. Yet Jesus replies using another word that Satan doesn't use—worship—exposing Satan's true intention. Jesus says straight out of God's word, "Worship the Lord your God, and serve him only" (Matt. 4:10).

Jesus knows what appears to be a slight nod in Satan's direction will turn into a lifetime of slavery. What Satan paints as a small act—bow down—is unmasked as cancerous servitude.

Have you traded your sense of integrity for a moment of entitlement? Have you given a small wink to Satan by choosing just for a moment to worship an earthly passion, only to find shackles clamped on your soul? Have you said yes to possessions that are now ruling your life, eating up your time, and destroying your peace of mind? What we sometimes overlook is the enormous upkeep involved with owning the kingdoms of this world and their splendor. It takes a great deal of time and money to polish, repair, dust, clean, mow, maintain, and weed these kingdoms. One day we wake up and realize that, along with all our stuff, we have an empty feeling, a sense that something is missing. Our mission and its satisfaction have disappeared.

The secret to walking with the Master in step with Wisdom is the ability to say no to temptation and yes to your essence. This is a well-defined mission statement.

Sometimes when I offer this section in a workshop or retreat, several people roll their eyes and mutter, "Oh, a mission statement." Their company has labored over one, or their sorority has spent countless hours designing a four-paragraph missive. Perhaps their church sent one through innumerable committees only to come up with something no one remembers.

Proverbs 4:25–26 is very clear about the power a mission statement holds for a wise woman's life: "Let your eyes look straight ahead, fix your gaze directly before you. Make level paths for your feet and take only ways that are firm."

At this point, I know my limits. I heartily refer you to *The Path* by Laurie Beth Jones. She artfully outlines the entire process to discovering our God-given passion. She explores the essential ingredients to a good mission statement. After reading and following the directions of *The Path*, you will have an excellent basic mission statement that will serve as a signpost, informing your daily activities and the choices you make. You will be able to discern the level paths and firm ways spoken of in Proverbs 4:25–26 as you fix your gaze directly before you.

A finished mission statement has three elements. I will outline my finished mission statement as an example of putting together the pieces of a puzzle.

First, you identify three verbs that grab your attention. A verb is an action word. What are the activities you seem to do no matter where you are? Do you teach, encourage, plan, support, motivate? Choose three of these and put them in place of the italicized words in the following example:

My mission is to *stimulate, encourage* and *celebrate*.

Secondly, a mission statement has a core value, that which you hope to bring about in the world as you pursue your three action words. Two word pictures may help tease this core value to the surface in you.

Throughout the Bible, God made a habit of renaming people to more genuinely reflect the character or destiny he had laid out for them. Abram was changed to Abraham, Sarai to Sarah. Cephas became Peter, and Saul transformed to Paul. If you were not named your current name, what value would you want your name to be? How would you like to be known? Joy, grace, faithfulness, peace, happiness, justice? When you walk into the room, people would say, "Oh, here comes . . ."

Or, if you could have just one word etched into your headstone to remind the world what you stood for, what would that word be?

My mission is to encourage, motivate and stimulate *the pursuit of wisdom.*

The final phase of this process is to discern what Jones calls your "tribe." Who are the people who have captured your heart, to whom you feel called to minister, who make your pulse quicken when you think of doing something that could change their lives? This could be an age group, a gender, a nationality, a sector of the public such as business or education, or your family. They are linked to your developing mission statement with the words *with, for, in,* or *to.*

My mission is to encourage, motivate and stimulate the pursuit of wisdom in *women of faith.*

Typically, when I take a group of people through this exercise, there is great groaning and sighing as they look through the lists, letting their truth bubble to the surface. Our ability to be and stay in touch with our true, created essence is consistently clouded by the daily activities and worries of life. To listen to our Creator, make wise judgments about the consistent threads that have run through our lives, and then determine that we will set our feet to the path we are discovering is hard work—right back to the stuff the sluggard hates! But as their picture develops, the group becomes more excited about getting in touch with what has been brewing all along—their essence and call. Embarking on and holding tightly to the truth of who we are and what we were created for is a critical difference between being dead as a fool and alive as a woman of wisdom.

Wise women also know that the path takes turns throughout life. Wise women are flexible. Wise women realize they can never impose their path on someone else. Proverbial Women are so busy strengthening their gifts, looking for good investments, doling out assignments, reverencing God, and uniquely providing for those they love, that they don't have time to be poking into anyone else's business. Wise women know they can always trust that, as they lean on God's gracious providence in the big picture and acknowledge God in every moment of every day, their paths and steps will be just where they ought to be.

That is peace, purpose, power. Put that in a brochure and mail it!

Your Proverbial Action Step

Assess and write down the three key elements of a personal mission statement noted in this chapter as they apply to you. Then take a look at your personal calendar to see how you are living out your mission and where there may be room for improvement.

CHAPTER FOUR

How to Have a Smart Mouth

The Proverbial Connection – *She speaks with wisdom and faithful instruction is on her tongue (Proverbs 31:26).*

Few things are more sickening than being caught in a lie. Unless perhaps, it's having a precious secret blasted throughout a group. Maybe it's worse to realize that you have crushed someone's spirit by speaking harshly to them in a moment of anger or frustration. A possible contender would be bragging about something you've done or obtained only to see the blank look of disinterest on other people's faces.

In Proverbs, there are more references to our communication habits than to any other topic mentioned. When seven sins are listed that the Lord finds detestable, three of them have to do with the little muscle in our mouths: a lying tongue, a false witness who pours out lies, and a man who stirs up dissension among brothers (Prov. 6:16–19). There is even a very graphic picture painted of females who don't know how to communicate wisely. "Like a gold ring in a pig's snout is a beautiful woman who shows no discretion" (Prov. 11:22).

The third chapter of James illustrates the power of our speech. A Proverbial Woman knows and understands the proper harnessing and use of this power.

> When we put bits into the mouths of horses to make them obey us, we can turn the whole animal. Or take ships as an example. Although they are so large and are driven by strong winds, they are steered by a very small rudder wherever the pilot wants to go. Likewise the tongue is a small part of the body, but it makes great boasts. Consider what a great forest is set on fire by a small spark. The tongue also is a fire, a world of evil among the parts of the body. It corrupts the whole person, sets the whole course of his life on fire, and is itself set on fire by hell. With the tongue we praise our Lord and Father, and with it we curse men, who have been made in God's likeness. Out of the same mouth come praise and cursing. My friends, this should not be (James 3:3–10).

Being a Proverbial Woman means every time you open your mouth you do so for the honor or dishonor of God; you show yourself to be a fool or a woman of wisdom. That's a pretty powerful load to bear, when you come right down to it. Little wonder Proverbs 10:19 and 20 counsels: "The more talk, the less truth; the wise measure their words. The speech of a good person is worth waiting for; the blabber of the wicked is worthless" (The Message). Perhaps it would be interesting to see what would happen to our wisdom quotient if we simply talked less and prayerfully considered all that comes out of our mouths!

The Top Ten Ways to Be a Woman of Proverbial Speech

1. Think before you speak. It happens every day in homes with small children. A youngster begins a sentence with, "I have a great idea!" Because of a schedule crunch or a tense mood in the home, mom or grandma will say, "Not now, honey." If that happens in my house, my daughter stamps her foot and says, "Mommy, you didn't even listen to what I was going to say." She's right. And sometimes when I get my head into the current moment and listen to what she has to say, it really is a great idea! It leads to something fun, or to the expedition of a task, or to a special moment together. Every time I do this, I think of the Proverb, "If one gives answer before hearing, it is folly and shame" (18:13).

Even more hurtful and foolish is barking a reply in a heated moment that causes the temperature to rise further. "A fool gives full vent to his anger, but a wise man keeps himself under control" (Prov. 29:11).

That experience is verifiable every time you sense you are getting into a disagreement with someone else, or you step into the middle of someone else's tangle. As an experiment for one month, try taking a deep breath, lowering your voice, and softening your eyes every time you feel the kettle brewing. See if it doesn't facilitate a better understanding between all involved.

Proverbs 15:28 says, "The heart of the righteous weighs its answers, but the mouth of the wicked gushes evil." Be a woman who thinks before she speaks, and forms a complete and loving answer. The best way to think before you speak is to be sure the other person has finished completely what they are saying in the first place.

2. Be an advocate. Wise speech meets loving service with world-changing results when you become an advocate for those who cannot speak for themselves. In Proverbs 31:8, King Lemuel's mother admonishes him, "Speak out for those who cannot speak, for the rights of all the destitute. Speak out, judge righteously, defend the rights of the poor."

Your speech is supremely wise when you use God's gift of your tongue to do the work of the Lord for peace and justice. Many people in our world, because of a handicap, age, or social disparity, cannot speak for themselves.

Who in your world cannot speak for himself, but is in need of mercy, justice, assistance or love? It could be you are called to champion the children of your church before a governing body. Maybe you are to promote the rights of someone you love as they lay dying or are in need of medical treatment. Does your elderly neighbor need an ally? Do the refugees on the television need an advocate? What's happening in the downtown area of your city or town? Is there a need for you to speak up for the rights of the poor, the undereducated, the imprisoned right in your own back yard?

Search your heart and see if part of your mission statement includes a ministry of advocacy.

3. Keep your promises. We don't like to think of breaking our promises as lying. It was an oversight; it slipped our minds; we just couldn't get to it. But Proverbs 12:22 has this word for would-be promise keepers: "Lying lips are an abomination to the Lord, but those who act faithfully are his delight." Faithfulness in our speech is evidenced when we say what we mean, and mean what we say.

My friend Karen told me about the difference a promise kept can make in a little person's life. She and her son went grocery shopping one evening. Part of that night's bounty was goodies for a packed lunch the next day. Michael was excited, looking forward to a special, homemade lunch.

The next morning, Karen's household, which includes a very busy husband and two other kids, was bedlam. Homework was flying into backpacks, hair was hastily brushed, cereal and milk were flowing at a rapid pace. There was simply no time to pack the much-anticipated expression of a mother's love, the lunch.

Michael went to the bus crying. Big tears flowed as he explained how much he had looked forward to this lunch full of the good things so carefully chosen the night before. My friend Karen has a real soft spot for her children, but she also had physical therapy and a lunch appointment with me that morning.

However, the more she thought about it, the more convinced she was that she needed to keep her promise to her son. She packed his little lunch box and drove nearly thirty minutes to deliver the precious promise to his private school classroom. She related later at lunch (which she was late for because of the promise delivery!), that she will never forget the look on his face when she walked into the room and handed him his lunch. Not only did Michael become convinced once more of his mother's love for him, he subconsciously reaffirmed that God is faithful and can be trusted.

4. Speak gently—Proverbs 15:1 says, "A gentle answer turns away wrath, but harsh words cause quarrels" (TLB). You have seen it in your own life. When you are provoked, but count to ten and speak gently to the one provoking you, the confrontation is more likely to be resolved than if you answered quickly in a harsh tone.

Taking on gentler speech as a regular habit will dramatically alter your everyday interactions. Those around you will realize you are not to be feared or dismissed because of a gruff or loud nature. We open the door to our brothers and sisters when we turn the knob with gentle ways and kind speech.

Whenever I present this in a seminar or retreat, I receive skeptical looks from the audience, many of whom have read books on assertiveness and getting what you want by speaking up and asking. There is nowhere in Proverbs that suggests we not be assertive or forthcoming with our feelings, opinions, and instructions. Proverbs does suggest that we never speak before we have assessed as much of the situation as we can, that we use a kind and gentle tone over a harsh and angry one, and that we make it short and sweet—in other words, worth hearing. You can convey the same words in a variety of tones with a predictable variety of results.

For example, my child can request a glass of milk in two very different ways. For one type of request, I would walk to the ends of the earth to milk an insane cow; for the other, I generally suggest she get milk from the refrigerator and pour her own glass.

Gentle speech makes your point in more ways than one.

5. Give wise instruction. Studying Proverbs gave me such good ammunition to use with my children. Nearly every day I wanted to quote to them Proverbs 1:8–9, "Listen, my son, to your father's instruction and do not forsake your mother's teaching. They will be a garland to grace your head and a chain to adorn your neck." This sounded pretty good. I can always use more scriptural backing to make my motherly points.

Then I realized, with a sickening thud, that a large part of Solomon's exhortation was based on the fact that I would offer words of instruction *worthy of hearing and heeding*. I actually had to have something nourishing and wise to say to my children as their instructor!

It was such a blessing when I recognized that the Book of Proverbs is a ready-made instruction manual for parents, teachers, grandparents, and other significant adults to use with the children entrusted to them by God. In specific, chapter four provides an insider's look at actual instruction offered by a parent. In general, Proverbs offers vivid word pictures, easy-to-understand illustrations, and often humorous examples to "impart moral wisdom and uncommon sense for right living" (Serendipity Bible, p.874).

We can be women of wise instruction when we carefully consider the person to whom we are speaking and prayerfully ask the Holy Spirit to help us recall relevant scripture or truth. Wisdom's promise resounds through Proverbs 3:6 once again, "In all your ways acknowledge Him and He will direct your paths." Hopefully it has already happened to you, that wonderful sense after a conversation that you were simply the mouthpiece for God's instruction, admonition, or encouragement. "A word aptly spoken is like apples of gold in settings of silver" (Prov. 25:11).

I have had the privilege of encountering two people who embody this kind of wise instruction. When Proverbial Women Ministries was in its infancy, I asked Dr. Jay Kesler, then President of my alma mater, Taylor University in Upland, Indiana, if he would give me an hour of his valuable time to hear my vision and offer direction. During our visit, he sat quietly while I articulated (and sometimes inarticulated) the ideas brewing in my soul. With great care and patience he listened, then said, "You know, I've been praying about what you're saying the whole time you have been talking so that I could offer you wise counsel and direction." What a gift! As he offered his insight and musings, I felt the conversation was anointed by the Holy Spirit and I knew I was the blessed recipient of wise instruction.

My other wise counselor is my colleague, Dr. Joan. With humor, unparalleled listening skills, and an ear for the Third Voice in every conversation, Joan has guided me through ideas and situations with great dexterity and wisdom. She embodies the Proverb. "The purposes in the human mind are like deep water, but the intelligent will draw them out" (20:5, NRSV). Whenever I have an idea for a project, seminar, or book, I go to Joan.

Joan attends with great interest. Then she does the most amazing thing. By asking a series of questions, and making suggestions of options I might want to consider, she helps me get a clearer picture of my path and my plan. Although she rarely gives direct instruction, she guides in such wise ways as she lets me know she trusts the unfolding Holy Spirit in my own life. She makes me a better person because she values and believes in me. Wise instruction pays equal attention to the value of the person and the value of the training.

6. *Speak honestly.* Honesty ranks first place in the number of proverbs given to its attention. In *The Message*, Eugene Peterson graphically sums up Proverbs 12:22 this way: "God can't stomach liars; he loves the company of those who keep their word." With good reason. People who are truthful clear the air (Prov. 12:17), bring enduring fidelity to all situations (12:19), save souls (14:25), are a delight to those in charge (16:13 and

22:11), stimulate affection and pleasure (24:26), and bring loving clarity to behavior and situations (27:6).

Some of us have no trouble telling the truth. We can tell the truth about anything, anybody, anytime. The only trouble is, we leave in our wake a string of bruised hearts and bleeding souls because of our harsh approach. On the other hand, some of us would be happy to tell the truth, except it might hurt somebody's feelings. It should come as no surprise that Proverbs 3:3 has advice for all of us when it comes to truth-telling. "Do not let kindness and truth leave you; bind them around your neck; write them on the tablet of your heart" (NASB). The wisdom of the sage is echoed years later when Paul admonishes the church at Ephesus, "God wants us to grow up, to know the whole truth and tell it in love–like Christ in everything" (Eph. 4:15, THE MESSAGE).

Bill Hybels, in *Making Life Work,* calls this the green zone, where truth and love come into perfect balance (p.95). I, being a Proverbial Woman in training, prefer to think of it as the purple zone (the color of the cloth she weaves and wears). Too much truth and I am decimated by the truth-teller. Too much love and there is no cutting edge offered for my authentic and necessary growth. When someone speaks to me, taking into consideration my identity as a sister in Christ and my own particular temperament and circumstances, when she offers suggestions and feedback to benefit me and my contribution to the kingdom, that person is speaking from the purple zone. As a person of wisdom, I need to listen to what this sage advisor has to say (Prov. 12:1, 15).

Living in the purple zone will be easier if we start with ourselves. "We need to understand that our commitment to honesty, first and foremost, has to do with telling *ourselves* the truth–and telling the truth *about* ourselves."[1] When we practice telling the truth in love to ourselves, we can do it more easily with others. Because we neither overinflate ourselves nor beat ourselves into the ground, we can be real, gentle, honest, and sometimes even humorous, with others.

7. Offer encouragement. Proverbs offers us at least three examples of what it means to be an encouraging woman.

"Congenial conversation–what a pleasure! The right word at the right time—beautiful!" (Prov. 15:23, The Message). Throughout the Old Testament, the blessing was the difference between life and death. To have a parent's blessing meant you could go forward in confidence; anyone who tried to defy you would find themselves in a pickle. The right word at the right time. Such a gift to be able to give, and such a treasure to receive.

"Pleasant words are a honeycomb, sweet to the soul and healing to the bones" (Prov. 16:24, NIV). Some people have it and some people have to cultivate it. My son, four-year-old Grant, just naturally has it. He has the uncanny ability to thank me or hug me at just the right time in my day. He is so pleasant and polite. When he says of his ham-and-cheese sandwich, "Thank you, Mommy, for this sandwich you made me," my heart is cleansed and whatever thought I was lost in evaporates as I drink in the wonderful elixir of someone appreciating what I have done. Or, out of the blue, eight-year-old Madison will sigh—with her head bowed over her homework— "I love you, Mama." I become completely refreshed, awash in the understanding that, regardless of the kind of Mommy I feel I really am, I am loved and those around me feel loved. Expressing appreciation and love are two highly encouraging ways for us to speak to others. Use them often and watch your world transform into the Kingdom come on earth as it is in Heaven.

"Like cold water to a weary soul is good news from a distant land" (Prov. 25:11). Often we can be encouraged by a phone call, email, or note that lets us know that someone far away is doing well, perhaps has recovered from surgery, has gotten a new job, has had a prodigal return home. This Proverb advises us to stay in touch with people we may not see all the time because of distance. In our society, so many families live far apart and a good word from a close-yet-distant relative can make someone's day. It is always encouraging to know someone thought of us, and that they are doing well.

8. Be humble. "Let other people praise you—even strangers; never do it yourself" (Prov. 27:2).

Les and Leslie Parrot, in *Like a Kiss on the Lips,* call this "being your partner's publicist" (p. 28). I have had the joy of knowing what they are talking about. One evening, while out to dinner with my husband and two gentlemen he was entertaining for work, he broke into a lovely description of Proverbial Women Ministries and what I was doing in its development. It was one of those moments when I fell in love with him all over again. He was proud of me, and he enjoyed what I was doing. What a gift!

You can be a publicist for others. Not giving false flattery, for Proverbs speaks of the insincerity of the flatterer, but an enthusiastic and heartfelt note of praise in front of others that uplifts and honors the one you are praising. When you do it as a surprise, so much the better. Let your children overhear you singing their accolades when you're talking with someone over the phone. Give a colleague a big verbal pat on the back in front of others.

Perhaps this is one thing King Lemuel's mother meant when she said, "She does him good and not harm all the days of his life" (Prov. 31:12).

"If you have played the fool and exalted yourself, or if you have planned evil, clap your hand over your mouth!" (30:33). Don't get yourself caught trying to make yourself look good; let other people do it for you. We will always come out shining when we let others tell of our strengths, good works, or insights. The temptation to brag ever-so-slightly is a sure path to enjoying our achievements less— not more—by leaving the aftertaste of empty self-promotion. How much better to receive an accolade from the mouth of someone else, and take genuine and humble pleasure from hearing the lovely words.

9. Make peace. With one of the rich rewards of wisdom being peace, it is little wonder plenty of proverbs guide us in using our tongue to bring peace to ourselves and those around us. The proverbs which on the surface seem to instruct in the ways of peace actually have more to say about gossiping. Gossips routinely destroy the possibility of peace in a situation because they are the wood which keeps the fires of strife burning (26:20) and they grab a passing dog by the ears (v.17). On the other hand, one who puts a stop to offensive talk and hurtful conversation is a person of peace and love–and great wisdom (10:10–13).

Some gossip is benign; it is honestly not meant to hurt others. When I sit at lunch with a friend and say, "You won't believe what my husband just did," it is an effort to connect with the sisterhood, to bond with my friend in joint incredulity at the ways of men. But I have taken a vow of faithfulness to my husband above all others, and I have broken that vow by telling something about him that he probably has not authorized. This may not seem like a big deal, except that it has sown two bad seeds. The first is that my friend now has a new lens through which to view my husband. Secondly, I have used my words to speak ill, when in the same space in time, with the same breath, I could have spoken words that brought peace and goodness into the world.

Another seemingly innocent practice is bringing a choice morsel (Prov. 26:22) you have discovered about someone you all know before your prayer group as a "prayer request." "I just found out this week that Julie has been let go from her job for some questionable practices." Julie does indeed need prayer. But before we bring something like this before a group, we need to ask Julie directly if she wants others to know about her situation. If she doesn't, you can hit your knees all you want on your own for intercession. If she does, maybe she can make a written request to the group or be more directly involved in asking for prayer. No matter how well-intentioned our motive when engaging in this practice, it is never right to bring up someone else's need to a group when we have not been confirmed to do so. It is gossip.

My internet tea buddy, Denise, shared with me two examples from her own life of women who have learned to harness this habit. "Believe it or not, my 17-year-old daughter comes to mind when I think of an example of wise speech. She does not participate in gossip or the trashing of 'friends.' She is weary of many of her classmates because of the habit of talking about those who are not present. She has never added to news I share about difficulties others are having . . . even when she has what could be thought of as 'the scoop' on others. She keeps prayer requests silent and private. She shares what truly will benefit others and not harm them.

"My grandmother, now deceased, was another example for me. She never said an unkind word about anyone. She comes to mind when I have a choice before me to share a prayer request that has private details with a mutual friend, or not at all . . ."

These are two ways that gossip slips out of our mouths even when we don't really mean to injure someone in the process. Other types of gossip are more overt and intended for hurt and division.

As justified as we might feel when someone has hurt us, or when we feel someone is clearly on the wrong side of an issue and we need to gather support, the way of wisdom commands that we keep our mouths quiet until we are truly searching for peace. Any division we have with someone is to be taken up directly with that person. A woman at a seminar once told me her Bible Study group was having a horrific struggle between the women who were staying home with their children and those who were working outside the home. She walked into a room where several members huddled around one particular member who was strenuously speaking against one of the other members who was not present. The absent member was in the "enemy camp" and the speaking member was seeking to gather support for her position against her sister. I have learned, through encounters like this on various topics, that God is less interested in where we come down on an issue than in how we treat others in the discussion. People are always more important than position.

Jesus didn't say we had to all agree on topics, but He did pray for our unity in spirit and in love (John 17:20–25).

As important as not gossiping is halting gossip when we encounter it. Proverbs offers two ways for us to do this. "Gossips can't keep secrets, so never confide in blabbermouths" (Prov. 20:19, The Message). Don't even give a confirmed gossip material to spread. Give them no logs for their fires. "You'll find wisdom on the lips of a person of insight, but the shortsighted needs a slap in the face" (10:13, The Message). I am not advocating we physically slap the offending gossip, but I am suggesting we take a proactive stance by calling the foolishness of the gossip's behavior as we see it. In private, of course, with love.

When it comes to gossip and peacemaking, Christ offered a wise and time-tested rule that has never failed us yet: "Here is a simple, rule-of-thumb guide for behavior: Ask yourself what you want people to do for you, then grab the initiative and do it for them. Add up God's Law and Prophets and this is what you get" (Matt. 7:12, The Message).

One of my favorite modern-day sages, Mary Englebreit, shared this in her 1999 Proverbial Calendar for the month of March:

There's so much good in the worst of us
And so much bad in the best of us
It ill behooves any of us
To talk about the rest of us.
> Julie's Grandma

10. Confess wisely. "You will never succeed in life if you try to hide your sins. Confess them and give them up; then God will show you mercy" (Prov. 28:13, TEV). When you have done something that needs confession, go directly to the person your transgression has offended. Make peace; accept forgiveness. One of my favorite images of confession is "run to the roar." When a group of lions is stalking prey, they designate one lion to stand up and roar, hopefully scaring the prey to run into the circle of lions lying in wait. If the prey will run to the roar, they are less likely ensnared by the hunters. In the same way, don't wait for your sin to come looking for you. When you know you need to confess, do it quickly and appropriately.

Appropriate confession means you involve only the parties who really need to know. Wise confession means a truthful accounting of wrong, apology for the consequences, an offer to make things right, and then turning from the transgression in the future. To "give up" the sin means to free yourself from the guilt and to let go of its practice in the future.

With the top ten of wise speech covered, there is one more very important piece of advice. Never underestimate the power of silence. "A man of knowledge uses words with restraint, and a man of understanding is even-tempered. Even a fool is thought wise if he keeps silent and discerning if he holds his tongue" (Prov. 17:27–28). Or as Abraham Lincoln said, "Better to remain silent and be thought a fool, than to speak out and remove all doubt."[2]

"When in doubt, don't" is a wonderful piece of folk advice I often use (although probably not often enough) when it comes to speaking or not. Any of us can look over our lives and rue the idiotic, cruel, misguided, or silly things we have said. This piece of wisdom need not take a lifetime to learn. If we learn and model for younger women this delicate and lovely characteristic, many tears and sleepless nights can be avoided. An anonymous quote I received by email said, "While we're learning to have a smart mouth, let's also train it to be quiet when the time is right."

One activity which helps keep our smart mouth quiet when the time is right is wise listening. Throughout Proverbs we are encouraged over a dozen times to embrace instructions (1:18), pay attention to experienced teachers (4:1), walk with the wise (13:20), seek counsel and sound advice (15:22), seek knowledge with our ears (18:15), and listen to the law (28:9). Perhaps this is why some have observed that we each have one mouth and two ears.

Discerning the difference between a sage and a fool is critical in wise listening. A thorough read of Proverbs will help us. Paying attention to the suggestions for wise speech give noteworthy instruction. As you are working on your own speech, you will begin to walk with the wise. These are the people through whom God can and will speak.

The benefits of seeking wise instructors are successful plans (15:22), increased wisdom (13:20), gaining complete information (18:17), and prayers that are heard and honored (28:9). The more we listen to and apply the guidance of wise counsel, the deeper and firmer our relationship grows with Lady Wisdom.

Which pounds are the hardest to take and keep off? The last ones just before you hit the target. Anyone who has dieted or trained will tell you the last few are the hardest to control. It's the extra stuff we put into our mouths and the exercises we skip that make the biggest difference.

Getting into spiritual shape is similar. There is always going to be something that is the biggest challenge in maintaining optimum spiritual fitness. For most of us it has to do with what comes out of our mouths and the control we fail to exercise over our words.

As we saw at the beginning of the chapter, the tongue is a pretty unruly creature. Usually when I teach this seminar, women seem to sink lower and lower in their chairs, burdened by the impossible load of taming the tongue. James 3:8 gives insight into a great comfort about our speech: "No human being can tame the tongue–a restless evil, full of deadly poison." At first blush this doesn't look much like encouragement, but the statement begs the question, "Well, who can?" Thanks be to God for the powerful gift of the Holy Spirit who can tame anything woman cannot. By the indwelling of and constant reliance on the Holy Spirit, we can count on our tongues serving us well and keeping us out of trouble.

Cut the fat out of your spiritual diet. Make a study of all the verses in the book of Proverbs that address wise speech. Start with one area at a time, conquer it with the help of the Holy Spirit, and then move on to the next. Exercise control over that tongue and experience the best spiritual shape of your walk with God!

Your Proverbial Action Step

Find ten 3X5 cards or pieces of sturdy paper. Write one of the ten ways to have a smart mouth on each card or paper. At the beginning of the first week, tape the first card to your mirror, refrigerator or computer monitor. Focus on that verbal attribute for one week. Replace the cards in the sequence at the beginning of each new week.

CHAPTER FIVE

The Service Advantage

The Proverbial Connection – *She opens her arms to the poor and extends her hands to the needy* (Prov. 31:20).

S he is in absolute anguish. She has fallen in love and has run away trying to make sense of the immense conflict between her devotion to God and her womanly instincts.

As is the wise thing to do, she seeks counsel from a trusted advisor, someone who walks in the Spirit of God and knows her very well. As the conversation unfolds and the emerging romantic love is revealed, the Reverend Mother says to a distressed Maria, "You have a great capacity to love. What we must find out is how God wants you to spend your love."

"But I've pledged my life to God. I've pledged my life to His service." Maria laments.

"My daughter, if you love this man, it doesn't mean you love God less."

At this turning point in the 1986 movie version of Rogers and Hammerstein's classic, "The Sound of Music," Maria is blessed with permission to meld her heart's longing with her profound desire to remain true to the service of God. She has discovered, with the help of an insightful and loving friend, that authentic service and God-given desires are best understood as sisters, not distant cousins.

The Proverbial Woman knows that service is not something she does, it is something she is. Grasping this distinction goes a long way in erasing some of the common objections as to why we "really can't serve right now." Remember, wisdom has more to do with character than performance. Performance can have faulty motives while pure character produces pure results.

Service comes out of living in tune with your mission and having cultivated a sense of gratitude and contentment. That is one reason service is such a challenge. It is hard work to cultivate gratitude and generosity sometimes. Often it boils down to sheer will-power and practice. When we are concerned with our own gain, as I described myself in the first chapter, it is spiritually impossible to allow service to flow from our hearts toward God and those we love. I had difficulty truly serving because I operated out of a sense of entitlement and a zero-sum view of life. There was only so much to go around, and if I didn't snag mine, it would be lost. Who had time for gratitude and contentment, much less true service?

I was busy making my place in the world. I needed to be noticed, and I really did not have time to waste on efforts that were not going to be applauded or recognized. But I could never be an authentic servant with that mindset. I didn't realize that I didn't need to carve out my niche. (Besides, nobody was really that impressed anyway.) My first hurdle was to realize, "These are the keys to servanthood. If we're confident of our place in God's family, we don't have to make a name for ourselves. If we're assured that we come from God and are called by God, we can be content to be invisible. If we are certain that our future lies with God, we don't have to exalt ourselves for our ultimate exaltation is already accomplished in Jesus Christ."[1]

Learning to serve has a way of completely changing our lives because it changes *us* in two important ways.

First, Proverbs 11:25 gives us a beautiful promise to ponder: "Your own soul is nourished when you are kind." When we feed the goodness in our hearts by having and sharing a spirit of generosity, we starve the negative forces inside. When we are kind, our soul feeds on that kindness and gets stronger, more fortified for more genuine service. Darkness subsides as light appears.

Secondly, our lives are changed simply because Christ knew exactly what He was talking about when He said, "In everything do to others as you would have them do to you" (Matthew 7:12, NRSV). He wasn't a parent wagging his finger at naughty children, He was a gracious sage who knew that if I am to treat others the way I want to be treated, a little seed of whatever it is I want to grow must first be planted in my heart. I already receive and have what it is I wish for others. God in His wisdom knew His instruction to love my neighbor as myself meant I would have to genuinely love myself first!

Even when our hearts are more in tune with God's call to service, we have several more questions.

The Proverbial Woman stretched out her hands to the poor and the needy. However, sometimes we can't get to the food pantry or the homeless shelter. With the overtime we're putting in, or the carpools we're driving, we cannot in our developmental phase minister to the overtly poor and needy. We must never make the mistake of thinking the poor and needy refers only to those in economic poverty. The woman in the next cubicle is poor in spirit; she is just aching for a good word. Your husband or significant other needs a safe place at the end of the day. Your child feels bad about the failed math test, and your neighbor needs an invitation to come to your house for chili sometime during the winter.

A huge question comes from wondering what we should do. "I'm only an accountant . . . or a mother . . . or a high school graduate . . . or a seamstress . . . or a shut-in."

First, Ephesians 2:10 tell us we were created for good works that God had established before we were born. The center of your service is wherever you are. God laid it all out for you from the beginning of time, while He was creating, with Wisdom by His side rejoicing over you (Prov. 8:31). So, each moment is a moment of service, each exchange is in God's name, and every loving action builds the Kingdom.

Secondly, there is a well-kept secret about service: you can actually enjoy it! It's OK to do something you feel called to do. Conversely, leave off your platter the things you don't feel an authentic, Spirit-filled tug to do. Let's be honest. You may have started on a project you thought you could squeeze into your schedule or learn to love, but at some point the grumpies took over and you asked yourself, "Why did I let them talk me into this?" Be creative in finding out what it is you like to do. Take your time in sorting through opportunities. Leave on the shelf the things you feel you ought to do and cannot do. Nobody wants to be around someone they look to for benevolence only to find a snarling, disgruntled "helper."

It goes back to the modified Microsoft question of chapter 2. When you look into the face of the Almighty early every day and ask, "Where do you want me to go today?" you set the stage for and enable an amazing, sometimes mysterious, series of opportunities and events. Every day becomes an adventure in which we lose ourselves and keep our eyes focused on the next enterprise presented by our loving Heavenly Parent. When we serve from our path, from our call, we do it happily, with anticipation, and a detachment from the outcome or reward.

Even when we are at peace with submitting to Christ's direction and are genuinely serving out of love, gratitude, and our essence, we can be overwhelmed by the world of need we face every day. Often, as I watch CNN or MSNBC, I am again astounded by the immense suffering of the hungry, the homeless, the oppressed, and the hopeless. What good does my life of service do to really change the world? In those moments, I have to remember that the breakfast I give my kids means the world to them. The clothes I clean out of my closet and take to church allow a teenager to go to school dressed, rather than dropping out for lack of covering. What you feel is a pitiful little offering may save someone's life. That's the beauty and mystery of partnering with God.

Another concern many have is becoming overwhelmed by the service we offer. We may overextend ourselves; people may expect too much of us; we may burn out. Proverbs 3:27 offers—you guessed it—wise advice as we make decisions on how much to extend ourselves: "Do not withhold good from those who deserve it, when it is in your power to act." The key phrase here is "when it is in your power to act." We are each bestowed with gifts and graces, but not any of us has them all. We are each given twenty-four hours a day, and nobody I know has yet found a way to be in two places at the same time!

When we feel overwhelmed, it's time to stop and ask, "What is on my plate? How did it get there? Are there any unhealthy motives for anything I'm doing?" There's a wonderful image of what happens when we try to hang onto things for motives other than the right one.

Do you know how monkeys are often trapped in the wild? The trappers construct a box whose slats are wide enough apart for the monkeys to slip a hand in, but not wide enough apart to pull it back out if they are holding onto something. Inside this box, the trappers place bananas. You get the picture. The monkeys reach inside, grab the banana and try to pull out their prize in their fist. They want the banana and they want to get away. Not willing to drop the bananas, the monkeys are then captured.

Whenever you are feeling trapped, smothered, or angered by service, decide to "drop the banana" of whatever motive has you snared. Keeping Proverbs 3:5–6 steadily before your eyes will go a long way in helping you see the box surrounding the banana. At the end of their conversation, the Reverend Mother told Maria, "You have to live the life you were born to live."

Finally, as with the Proverbial Woman's example of her relationship with her husband, we can never underestimate the power of the support we bring to others who are serving. I call this indirect service. We can take vicarious satisfaction in the service of others whom we are serving behind the scenes. Our covert service to them allows them to render overt service to others.

A dear indirect service role model for me is my mother. Having served directly for many years as a public school teacher and a mental health professional, my mother has now answered a call to a less public service role as she daily gives my preschool son Grant an extraordinary childhood. My husband and I are enabled to direct service in the church by her service. My mother is living proof that you can enjoy the service to which God has called you. And my son is highly blessed, indeed.

One of the most beautiful servants I have ever met shared her secret of joyful, genuine service. She always looked for the unfolding Christ in each person and vowed to serve Him through them in whatever way presented itself at that moment.

Mother Teresa, legendary for her service said:

Don't look for spectacular actions.
What is important is the gift of yourselves.
It is the degree of love you insert in your deeds.[2]

Make up a game with yourself to see how many wonderful things you can find to do in secret, then do them. Make service a way of life, not an isolated project. Little things done in private can make a big difference in the big picture.

"The noblest service comes from nameless hands, and the best servant does his work unseen."[3]

Your Proverbial Action Step

Make a list of ten acts of service you could secretly do this month. Do them.

CHAPTER SIX

Wise Laughter

The Proverbial Connection – *She is clothed in strength and dignity, and she can laugh at the days to come* (Prov 31:25).

T he doctor says there's a little spot she wants me to have checked out by a specialist. I didn't really want to tell you until you got home, but I guess I just had to let you know." My husband spoke those words to me on the Sunday of a long weekend while I was on a little jaunt to Florida with two girlfriends. He was in his Indiana hometown with our two kids and this was the first time since Friday that we had connected. As my pounding heart and churning stomach tried to grasp what he was telling me, the worst scenes budded and then burst into full bloom in my racing mind. Not only was my heart sick over the thought of losing my soul mate, my beloved,

I realized what a poor steward I had been of my resources on many levels.

Did I know where all of our finances stood? Had I built the kind of relationships with my kids that could withstand the test of me being their only parent? Did my husband know beyond any doubt how truly special and dear he was to me? Was the house in good repair? Had I made wise investments into my support system in case I needed to draw on the interest now? Had I spent my time discerning my path, my mission that would transcend the role of wife and at the same time provide for my family? Was my own faith strong enough to weather this storm? I'll tell you one thing, I didn't feel strong and dignified, nor was I laughing.

Our friend and mentor, the Proverbial Woman, could laugh at the days to come because she was a good steward. She took care of the clothing in her home. She kept herself strong. She made sure her family was gainfully occupied. She invested the money she made from her entrepreneurial efforts.

Good stewardship is one way God laughs with us—as His ends are accomplished through us by the outpouring of His provision and our prudent usage. Second Corinthians 9:8 gives a radical accounting of God's economy: "God is able to make all grace abound to you so that in all things at all times having all that you need, you will abound in every good deed." This does not suggest that perhaps if God is in a good mood, or if I've been a particularly good girl, possibly God will give me a tad of grace to half-way do a job that may benefit someone. The word "abound" is used twice and "all" is used four times. It is a passage just gushing with possibilities, if I learn how to tap into God's accounts and use well what I find flowing through me on a constant basis.

The Proverbial Woman was the consummate steward. She understood the spiritual laws in God's economy. The more you appreciate what you have, the more you have. The more you use what you have, the more you find you have. The more you care for and cultivate what has been given to you, the more will come your way. The more joy and satisfaction you bring to your world, the more you bring to yourself. The more you trust in God to guide you, the more you feel that guidance. Stewardship is an issue of trust.

In what ways did this woman allow God to laugh through her as she trusted in Him for protection and provision? What do they mean for us as contemporary Proverbial Women?

"She selects wool and flax and works with eager hands" (Prov. 31:13). As part of her stewardship, this woman made sure she had the very best materials to work with to create the best quality product she could. Because she had chosen good resources, she was excited about her work and what she would produce. If part of our call involves working with our hands in a craft, it means we use the best materials we can find to ensure that our product can be a lovely example of fine raw materials encountering the master's touch. If your call requires training, get the best you possibly can to make the most of what you have been given.

In her stewardship, she knows that her budget and procurement needs to allow for some special surprises for her household. "She is like the merchant ships, bringing food from afar" (v. 14). When we are grocery shopping, we can look for the best quality food that our budget will allow.

We can also seek out those special little treats that bring a smile to someone's face when they realize it's a bit out of the ordinary.

She took administration seriously. Verse 15 tells us she stayed ahead of the game with her family. She anticipated when they would need to eat and prepared for this. This Hebrew woman also had servant girls in her household. She saw to it that their work kept them gainfully busy and aided in the overall management of the home. Today we have dishwashers, washing machines, dryers, and ovens to act as our servant girls. One of our tasks may be to see that our machines are all properly and effectively used. When it comes to cleaning, I don't personally feel the need to do all the household chores myself, but I am a good steward of my family's energy when it comes to straightening up the house.

As part of the domestic administration of her household, this woman guaranteed that her children were occupied. "She watches over the affairs of her household" (v. 27), indicates that if she were living today, she probably oversaw homework, signed permission slips, taught the children how to launder their own sports uniforms, and kept the family calendar under control. She may have offered advice to lovelorn teenagers or heartbroken ex-best friends. She knew where her family members were and when they were coming home. She had an eye for the talents, interests, and skills of each person in her family, and she played to their strengths. She was the central nervous system of the family.

She kept herself in good shape. "[H]er arms are strong for her task" (v. 17b). This physical strengthening has one motive—to help her efficiently carry out her tasks, oversee her investments, and effectively manage her entire household. What a relief in our body-conscious society. So often we are obsessed with staying in good form or depressed when we don't feel we measure up. The amount of exercise we need is the amount it takes to keep us in optimum shape to carry out our mission. The focus is on our health, not our physique.

Not to be confused with the vanity of beauty, and not in contradiction with the previous paragraph, she also exhibited stewardship over her appearance. Her physical presentation was congruent with who she knew herself to be as God's gift to her family and community. Part of her entrepreneurial endeavor was making linen garments and selling them; she supplied sashes to the merchants. Representing herself and her pride in her work, she herself wore fine linen and purple which she had made. She produced her own clothing and was joyfully pleased with what she produced. Whatever your mission is, dress appropriately, comfortably, and in a way that is authentic to your personality. Look deep into your motives regarding clothing style and appearance and make them as pure as possible. Then dress according to your strengths and God's glory!

Proverbs 31:25 mentions two other wardrobe items she wore regularly: strength and dignity. As important as, if not more so than, what she arrayed herself with outwardly, was the internal raiment she chose from the wardrobe of characteristics. Keeping our spiritual clothing clean and in good repair will do more to keep us beautiful and attractive than any spa treatment and make-up lesson.

The Proverbial Woman kept a close eye on the finances. She was an entrepreneur making full use of the gifts God had given her to bring financial support to her family. She was a speculator, looking at and buying land, and used the money she had earned to reinvest in a field. She was a smart businesswoman who kept her eye on the marketplace and knew "the value of everything she made" (v. 18). Her esteem of her work kept her energized to work late into the night. She loved to work and took pleasure in providing products that would benefit the community and enrich her family. Our finances are simply one more gift to be managed with wisdom. We need to keep an eye on the value of our products and services so we are adequately compensated while not over-inflating our worth and damaging our ability to minister in the community. When we are doing what we love and feel we are earning a fair wage (if wage is part of the package), we find energy to work hours the normal, unmotivated worker would not consider. It flows from who we are, a God-given grace we extend to others.

Her stewardship encompassed her household possessions. She knew good stewardship meant taking care of what she had, such as keeping the clothes in good repair (v. 21). When you provide good maintenance, you spend less money in the long run in more costly repairs. One of my dear friends regularly wears clothing she has had for over a decade. She has two secrets to its longevity: she buys classic clothing that is well made, and she cares for her clothing with tenderness and attention. Another friend provides consistent and complete maintenance for her cars. She is able to drive a car long after it has been paid for, freeing up money in the budget for other things while she has good, dependable transportation for years. When possible, the optimum combination for stewardship of our material things is to purchase the best we possibly can, then keep things in good condition through routine and tender care.

A true test of stewardship is what we do when resources are scare. Sometimes we have to exhibit the faith of Christ in the feeding of the multitudes. We must trust in God's ability to produce the impossible through our willingness to lay our seemingly meager assets in His hands. God seems to delight in people of trust as He makes a memorable example of their faith. Patsy Clairmont remembers, "My mom could do anything, especially with her hands. Organize, customize, or economize, she could do it all. She could take a shack and transform it into a cottage. She could take a chicken and concoct a feast, and she could take a nickel and create a bankroll. I don't know how she did what she did with what she had, but perhaps growing up in a large family on a farm, living through the Depression, and marrying a milkman gave her the opportunity to be creative, versatile, resourceful, and industrious."[1]

The stewardship of our time is one of the most telling ways of measuring our trust. When you have done the hard work of chapter 3 and know your mission clearly, you've gone a long way in assuring that you are a good steward of the 24 hours of each day that God has given you. You will not make promises of your resources that are off your path. Being fully assured that God is in control of every situation and has created an answer for every need, you can be freed by knowing that it is someone else's mission to teach Sunday school, head the PTO, sew for the homeless shelter downtown, or raise money for the new organ. But sometimes, for a variety of well-meaning reasons, we say yes to a task or commitment we really wish we had said no to. Proverbs offers very helpful coaching for those who find themselves caught in the poor stewardship of their promises and pledges. Go humbly to those to whom you made the pledge and extract yourself as quickly and thoroughly from the pledge as possible. In this way you "Free yourself, like a gazelle from the hand of the hunter, like a bird from the snare of the fowler" (Prov. 6:5).

Good stewardship is really a contentment issue. When we are content, we are not grasping for the next thing, the newer or bigger or neater thing. Fully embracing what has graciously been given to us, we are free to lovingly care for it and joyfully share it.

Are we content with how our children are (apart from the little rough edges that need constant sanding)? Do we genuinely enjoy the clothing we have? Are we amused and amazed by our own talents and gifts? Have we made peace with our household budget? Are we happy with ourselves and the precious corner of the world God has assigned us to serve? Anything in life that we have been given, whether it be time, talent, or treasure, is a gift from God. When we are content, we take better care of what we have. When we are free from our "wanting" mind, we can focus on the abundance already there and share it freely—knowing we will always be cared for by our loving Heavenly Provider, whom we will never outgive.

Good stewardship is summed up in a provocative story I received from a friend via email. It seems Satan held a convention with all of his evil angels. They bemoaned the fact that they can't keep Christians from reading their Bibles, going to church, or holding certain values. But Satan devised a plan nonetheless. If they could keep Christians so busy that they couldn't pursue an authentic relationship with God, they could win a great share in the battle.

He instructed his angels to keep humans busy in the non-essentials of life. He told them to get humans to spend, spend, spend; then borrow, borrow, borrow. To top that off, humans should be drawn to work long hours, keeping parents away from their children and fragmenting families just to pay for their overextended credit limits.

Their second line of attack was overstimulating human minds with television, PCs, the internet, radio, CDs and VCRs. Even listening to and watching neutral material would crowd out the best, the still small voice, thus weakening the power of God's Holy Spirit in their lives.

Next came the ambush of reading material: catalogs and mountains of junk mail, magazines, and newspapers. All kinds of promotional materials offering peace, prosperity, and power for a small fee.

The last assault would come from twisting the gift of the Sabbath to such an extent that recreation would even be excessive. Sporting events, cultural events, and media events should leave humans exhausted and unprepared for living from their center. The angels were instructed to infiltrate fellowship gatherings, inciting humans to gossip about those who were absent, and involving them in so much small talk that they would leave troubled and unsettled but wouldn't know why.

The devil went so far as to suggest that Christians be allowed to talk to others about God, to attempt to be a witness. However, the evil angels should allow them to fill their lives with so many good causes that they wouldn't have time for the Source and would go through all the motions under their own strength, eventually sacrificing their relationships and their health.

The point of the story hit home as I looked around my house one day to see the housework undone, the calendar full, the schoolwork in various locations, and the family crabby. Taking control of our situation and being good stewards does not restrict the movement of God's

Spirit. Taking control to clear the confusion, orchestrate the noise, harness the resources, and focus on the essentials actually allows more quiet for the voice of God to speak. It allows space for the Spirit to freely flow and transform. As one of my friends once said, "When the devil can't make me bad, he makes me busy." Take control of your world to allow God greater control in your life.

As seen earlier in the chapter, the Proverbial Woman's stewardship of her relationships yielded terrific benefits. One of the greatest blessings was the laughter she must have had with her family. Her children were vocal about their love for her. Her husband spoke glowingly and publicly about his esteem for her above all others. What made her such a treasure in their eyes? She was aware that she was God's gift to them and handled herself with generosity and effectiveness. Read on.

Your Proverbial Action Step

On a piece of paper list all of your resources. Include emotional, financial, spiritual, relational, physical, and attitudinal. On a scale of 1 to 10, with 1 being horrible and 10 being outstanding, rate your stewardship of those resources. Where do you go from here?

CHAPTER SEVEN

You are God's Gift for Others

The Proverbial Connection – *Her children arise and call her blessed; her husband also, and he praises her: 'Many women do noble things, but you surpass them all'* (Prov. 31:28–29).

Have you ever compared yourself to someone else? How did you fare? How did the other person come out? Funny thing about comparisons, someone always loses! If you perceive the other person to be better than you are, you lose. If you perceive yourself to have the advantage, the other person loses. Not only is esteem lost, but the opportunity to be an authentic peer with that person, to find out all the wonderful things God is doing in her life and to see what partnerships you could be forging, is lost.

Becky Freeman, in her September 1999 address to the Women's Conference "A Day Away," said that one mark of a highly real woman is her awareness that she is uniquely loved by God. To revisit the basic foundation of this book, you are deeply, passionately, and eternally loved by God. Not only does God love you, God likes you.

Still, we sit in Bible study or women's fellowship, or stand in line at the department store check-out or the back-to-school ice cream social and compare ourselves to others. Being women, we most likely are not comparing favorably, so we ask, "Why am I here?" "Was God just kidding when he made me?" "Why can't I be more like so-and-so?"

You have very good company in a beautiful queen from the Old Testament. Queen Esther's mission was to save the Jewish people from complete annihilation. To accomplish this she had to approach her husband, the Persian king, without being summoned. To go into his presence without an invitation was certain death. While preparing herself spiritually and physically for several days, she consulted her gatekeeper uncle, Mordecai. He wisely encouraged her with the beautifully poetic question, "Who knows if you have not attained royalty for such a time as this?" (Esther 4:14b, NAS)

You are the mother God has sent to your children, the friend He sent to your friends, the wife to your spouse, the employee to your colleagues. It is no mistake that you are who you are and where you are at this point in history and in this place on the planet.

The perfect gift has three key elements.

First, the gift is well-timed. I am a quilter and many of the gifts I have given in my life are quilts. A well-timed gift means the quilt I construct for a baby gets to the child before she enters college. Gifts have their maximum impact when they are given at the proper time, not too early and not too late.

Secondly, the gift takes into consideration the tastes and needs of the recipient, as well as the occasion for the gift. Several years ago, my dear friend Theresa had her second child. Within minutes it became obvious that the tiny boy was in severe distress. Within hours we knew that his heart was not functioning properly. Within a week he received a transplant of a tiny, walnut-sized heart. To celebrate Sam's spirit and God's faithfulness, I chose a quilt block of pastel-colored hearts set in primary-colored balloons. Members of our bible study and mom's groups signed each quilt block with praises and continued prayers for Sam's health and growth. I take the quilt with me whenever I speak on this topic. Sam has grown enough that he knows his life and his quilt are special in God's work. When God sent Jesus, he took into account our human nature, our sinfulness, and the Christ-shaped hole each of us has in our lives. God's gifts are perfectly designed.

Thirdly, a gift should be so well-done that the creator and/or giver should be proud to put her name on it. I sign and date each quilt. A famous basket-making mill in Ohio has all the weavers initial and date their creations. God's handwriting was all over Jesus.

God's handwriting is all over you, as well. One autumn Sunday morning, as I made my rounds as Director of Children's Ministries at the church I was serving, I peeked into the three-year-olds' room. They were sitting on the floor, enraptured, as the teacher recounted the days of creation. She said, "And on the fourth day, God created day and night." One sweet little cherub piped up, "Well, that was a good idea!" In the same way, I imagine God crossing His arms proudly over His chest after forming each of us and saying, "Now that was a good idea!"

But not all of us are ready, willing, or able to embrace and celebrate that we are God's gift to others. Dysfunctional parenting, our basic sin nature, physical flaws, unattainable magazine covers, or failed attempts to be something or someone, may have convinced us that we are not worthy, lovable, or useful to anyone. What happens when we experience this kind of setback?

I am a walker. Three times a week, I like to get out for a vigorous walk using some praise music I have found specially designed for striders. One early summer midmorning, I was out exercising at the height of my aerobic capacity when the strangest thing happened. The music started slowing, the singing got sluggish, and every walker's sadness occurred. The batteries in my tape player died. My music was gone, my rhythm was gone, my guide was gone. I just gave up and went home.

Each of us has internal music, a God-given symphony we are intended to play. We each have our voice in the choir, and if we are absent, the whole song will not work.

Spiritual gift inventories abound and they are often helpful in putting the puzzles together for a particular portion of the Body of Christ as they seek to work together. We can tell if we have the gift of prophecy, hospitality, administration, or others identified by these tests. While it is certainly helpful to know what gifts we have, we must never lose sight of the gift we are.

There are three ways we impact the world with the gift of who we are. In the remainder of this chapter, we'll take a look at time, truth and 'tude.

Time. Time as a gift is assessed in two ways: time with and time on.

When you spend time with people, you let them know you not only love them, but you like them as well. We all need to know we are liked. Young children feel this quite keenly. My college roommate, Vicki, told me of a time when she said to her mother, "Mommy, do you like me?"

"Why yes, honey, you know I love you very much."

"But Mommy, do you *like* me?"

"Honey, Daddy and I both love you!"

Finally, an exasperated little girl said, "But Mommy, do you *like* (foot stomp) me?"

At last her mother understood and said, "Of course honey, I like you very much."

We'll look at three ways in particular to spend time with people, but there are hundreds to discover. Those are up to your imagination, inspiration, and individual situation.

Praying with someone else has the power to unlock the gates of heaven and shower you both with blessings. Jesus commented on the power of at least two in prayer. "Again, I tell you that if two of you on earth agree about anything you ask for, it will be done for you by my Father in heaven. For where two or three come together in my name, there am I with them" (Matt. 18:19–20).

One morning a dear friend came into my office to give me an update on some conditions in her life. Near the end of our brief time, I asked her if we could pray together. In the midst of our prayer, I welled up with gratitude for her and the use of her plentiful gifts in the ministry of our church. I was truly thankful for her life.

Several days later a beautiful card came in the mail. It read, "Thank you so much for your friendship! You are such a blessing to me and my family! Talking and praying with you yesterday morning helped me in ways I can't even explain. Such peace you shared! I have never had anyone pray a prayer of thanks for *me*–it felt awesome! Thank you for taking the time to share God's Grace."

I was struck by two things about this card. First, it only took five minutes of time for us to have our conversation. The Holy Spirit is so present and eager to be involved that His activity can be experienced in something that takes just moments. Secondly, in thirty-plus years of living, she had never heard anyone pray a prayer of thanksgiving for her. Praying with people should be a regular part of everyday life as we invite God's presence into everything we do and are.

We need to spend time touching those we love. Studies show we need at least 13 hugs a day to stay healthy. My husband is a marriage and family therapist. In his marriage retreats and premarital seminars, he encourages couples to take time each day for a 30- second hug and a 7-second kiss. Young children learn to read better when they are sitting securely with someone they love. They feel secure enough to take their time in sounding out words and correcting mistakes.

Jesus knew the power of spending time with people at special occasions. He attended weddings, funerals, and dinner parties. The invitation to my fortieth birthday party began, "In celebration of God's grace and the gift of your friendship." I realized as I reflected on 40 years of living that I had been blessed with hordes of friends and an amazing family. I wanted to rejoice! The evening was full of cake and coffee, the laughter of children, many hugs, and an occasional "remember Robin when" story. I will never forget the people who were there. Many brought lovely gifts, but their presence was a memorable treasure. "The toys and the presents will soon fade away, but they'll never forget the gift of a day."[1]

On the other end of the occasion spectrum is the unforgettable gift you give when you spend time with someone who is grieving. At a particularly difficult service for a young man who left behind three children and a stunned widow, I stood in line with a lovely woman who mused, "I just don't know what to say." Having been in pastoral ministry, I could assure her that our friend was in such a condition that she really did not hear the words we said, but keenly felt our presence and our hugs. When people are grieving, they need genuine people around them offering authentic support and the necessary space and time to mourn and heal. There are times when words are elusive, but a heartfelt hug or a pat on the hand say what the most carefully crafted phrases cannot.

It is no small struggle to give this gift of time *with*. It requires sacrifice and some careful planning to get everything done. But the benefits to both the giver and the recipient are evident in this wonderful poem by Brenda Clapp.

As I was folding laundry one day,
The telephone began to ring.
While I was talking on the phone, I noticed
The dishwasher needed unloading.

So, as I started to unload the dishwasher
And talked on the phone
My five-year-old loudly requested
An ice cream cone.

As I served the ice cream
And finished my call,
I remembered I had a shower gift
To get at the mall.

I shuffled through the kitchen junk drawer
Now where is the coupon for that department store?
Ding-dong! Someone was at my front door.
And now, ice cream, all over my floor.
Be angry, sin not, I thought as I went to the door.
"Whoever said that," I mumbled,
"hasn't seen this messy floor."

"Ma'am, would you like to buy a candy bar
to support a good charity?"
"Of course, I'll get my purse,"
but finding it quickly would be a true rarity.

"Can you wait just a minute?"
I said to the boy.
My purse could be anywhere in the house,
My daughter thinks it's a toy.

I paid the young man and thought to myself,
Weird fashion these days, to wear pants so droopy.
Upon closing the front door, my two-year-old yelled,
"Mommy, I'm poopy."

I made my way up the cluttered stairs,
To find a clean diaper was my goal.
I tripped over a Barbie
And down the stairs it did roll.

For crying out loud! I thought to myself,
I think I've put that doll away twice!
"&%#$%," I said under my breath,
Such language, although said quietly, what a terrible vice.

Forgive me, Lord, for the things I think and say.
I guess I'm a little harried today.
I promise to keep my frustration at bay.
Seeking your counsel always makes things okay.
I'll remember that next time my nerves start to fray.
Now . . .what did I come upstairs for anyway?

During my short prayer
At the top of the stairs,
I spied my daughter's bedroom
All cluttered with dolls and stuffed bears.

"What a zoo!" I exclaimed,
and began making the bed.
Suddenly, "Mommy, where are you?" I heard,
"What is it?" I said.

Then I saw her doing
Her dirty diaper dance.
Amidst praying and bedmaking,
I'd forgotten to change her pants.

Is it bedtime yet? I wondered,
As I changed the dirty drawers.
I really do need to finish
All of these household chores.
I don't have much trouble starting the work,
That's true,
It's completing the task
That is so hard to do.

My daughter stood up
And gave me a great hug.
Her sloppy kisses always give
My heart strings a tug.

I guess all this housework
Will just have to wait.
I want to play with my kids
Before it's too late.

"They grow up so fast,"
my mother would say.
"Before you know it, you'll be asking
for their attention someday."

We did puzzles, colored pictures
And played all afternoon.
Frankly, for the first time,
I thought bedtime came too soon.

After teeth brushing, book reading
And prayers were all said,
My kids were safely, soundly, happily
Tucked in to bed.

I surveyed the unfolded laundry, dirty dishes
And sticky floor.
"How was your day?" my spouse asked,
As he came through the door.
"Oh honey," I answered,
"You know how some days are,
the only thing I finished today
was a chocolate candy bar."

Just as it was in spending time *with* people, prayer is at the top of the list of ways to spend time *on* people. When we spend time on people in prayer, we gift them in ways that are mysterious, powerful, and often known only to God. Although it may seem futile, unfruitful, and like shooting in the dark, uplifting people the Holy Spirit lays on your heart at seemingly odd times is cooperating with the Almighty in bringing His kingdom to earth. How often has God lain someone on your heart, and when you mention it to them they respond that they were, indeed, in need and were blessed to know you had thought of them?

Equally important is consistent, daily prayer for God to bless, teach, and guide the special people in your care. These fortunate, albeit often unknowing, recipients of your constant efforts on their behalf may be children, parents, spouses, friends, or colleagues and neighbors for whom you are concerned.

Sometimes we run out of "material" when praying for these loved ones. After seven weeks of "Please bless Susie," we may long for meatier prayers that change the world because they change us and the people for whom we are praying. "The Bible is a great vehicle for focusing our communication with the Lord," says Cheri Fuller.[2] Choosing

Scripture passages to meditate on and claim for people we love can be fun, rewarding, and bring surprising results. This practice aids our deeper understanding of the Word. It helps us stay alert for specific ways our prayers are being answered.

Several terrific passages to consider for this practice are Colossians 1:9–14 or 3:12–17, Ephesians 3:14–21 or 16:10–18, or 1 Corinthians 9:10. You might even choose passages in Proverbs and pray particular wisdom to come into the lives of those you love! The real trick in this kind of prayer is to blanket the person in your requests and leave the details up to God.

Which envelopes do you open first when shuffling through the mail? Is it the envelope marked "Resident," or the one with your name typewritten on it? Do you eagerly dive into the package that promises to be a bill or a solicitation for yet another credit card? If you're like most people I've surveyed, the first piece of mail that captures your attention is the hand-addressed, pretty envelope bearing the return address of someone you love. To read a nice wish from a friend or a lovely piece of news from a dear family member simply warms the heart and brings a smile to the face. Even if the note bears a poem or sentiment penned by another author, you know when you receive it that sometime a few days earlier, someone spontaneously thought about you. Maybe they were standing in the store and grabbed a card for you. Perhaps they were having some quiet time and your name popped into their head and they knew they had to drop you a quick note. Maybe they saw something on television or heard a piece of music that they knew you would love. Whatever the circumstance, they not only thought of you, they took the time to write a thoughtful note that would touch your heart several days later.

One afternoon, my kids thought I had lost my mind. As I sifted through the mail, I got excited and then cried in the span of five minutes. My precious friend Claudia had sent not one, but two special treats in an envelope! The first was a note handwritten on a simple card thanking me for our friendship and looking forward to our next time together over coffee. The second was a tiny little card with "Faith" etched into the sand of the seashore on the cover, and a beautiful little quote inside. Claudia has three talented, active children, at least 14 pets, and a flourishing marriage to a gifted physician. She does not have lots of discretionary time in her day. But without having any special reason, except for her kind thoughtfulness, she took time to send me a heartfelt celebration of friendship. She is a gift.

Just imagine how different your life would be if once each week you sent a heartfelt note to someone who has meant something to you. You would send out gifts of love and memory to special people in your life. Since "you reap what you sow," imagine all the goodness that would come back your way. The most wonderful thing about giving this kind of gift is that it can be done by those who are house bound, it takes just a few moments to do, and costs almost nothing.

A final way to spend time on people is to leave a legacy. In chapter 4, I introduced a conversation I had with Dr. Jay Kesler at Taylor University. As he and I became acquainted, I introduced myself as a former Taylor student and friend of his son. While I am certain he found that impressive, what brought the light of recognition to his eyes was realizing who my relatives were. "Oh, your grandfather is Loyal Ringenberg. He's one of my heroes. That must mean your uncle is Bill Ringenberg [a history professor on campus]. So you are the daughter of Walt and

Lenore Chernenko. We went to school together. Your father was a steady, stable man of God." How grateful I was
that my ancestors had behaved themselves! It reminded
me of Joshua 24:13: "So I gave you a land on which you
did not toil and cities you did not build; and you live in
them and eat from vineyards and olive groves that you
did not plant." Those who had gone before me had paved
the way for me to walk a well-padded path. Even if your
relatives did not smooth the way for you, you can still see
yourself as a gift in this way. Your Christ-like living is
sowing fertile seeds for those in your family who are coming after you. Just be who you are as you watch God's
plan develop in your life and watch the generations unfold in power and prosperity.

Preserving and retelling your family history are immeasurable gifts to those around you as well. My entire
family, including grandparents and siblings, love poring
over family albums that not only have pictures in them,
but journaling and storytelling woven among the photo-
graphs. One of my children's favorite bedtime activities is
snuggling on the couch under a quilt and playing, "Tell
me a story about when I was a baby." They love hearing
their own story and delight in the retelling of funny and
embarrassing antics. They find true pleasure and soul satisfaction in hearing tales of their tenderness and discovery. Give the generations the gift of their heritage, com-
munal and individual.

Truth. Chapter four had a great deal to say about telling
the truth. As we look at the gift of truth you give to others,
we focus on what it means for you to *be* the truth. While
Jesus stated numerous times in the gospels, "I tell you the
truth," one of His most shocking and controversial claims

is that He *was* the Truth (John 14:6). Why was Jesus the Truth? One reason is He completely and without hesitation understood and lived out His mission. He was authentic; He was the earthly representation of His Heavenly Father. He knew exactly what His music was and how to live it out in each day.

When we are truthful, people can trust us. The truth has a way of bonding people together. John 8:32 says, "You will know the truth and the truth will make you free." When you are immersed in the truth of God's deep, passionate and eternal love for you, you are then free of public opinion, recriminating ghosts of the past, and all the little communication prisons we face every day. Henry David Thoreau said, "Between whom there is a hearty truth, there is love."[3] There is love because nothing feels so good in all the world as being completely ourselves and feeling completely accepted. When you are in the presence of a truthful person, you can relax. You leave your meeting with her saying, "I'm a better person for having been with her."

Are you authentic in the way you live? Are you for real? Do you wear each day what you love to wear, or do you dress for the neighbors, the others in Bible Study or the mall walkers? Do your volunteer activities reflect heartfelt passions, or are they social climbing maneuvers? Are your children involved in activities that are "training them up in the way they should go" (Prov. 22:6), or are they doing what the "in" crowd does so they (and you) won't be left out? Are you comfortable with your path and your identity as a deeply, passionately, eternally loved daughter of God, or are you putting up a front to make people think you are who you hope to be (or think you should be)?

When we embrace the music God has gifted us with, when we let those patterns and fabrics God carefully crafted shine through our unique personality, we can move gleefully and confidently through our days. We will sleep peacefully, as well.

Hans Christian Anderson tells a remarkable story of two characters who changed their community. In *The Emperor's New Clothes* we meet a royal clotheshorse who is so vain all he can think about is the next outfit he's going to parade in front of his loyal subjects. Two con men pass through the kingdom to offer their assistance in suiting his royal highness in threads that are so magnificent only the wise and informed can see them. They work for weeks, all the while inviting in the king's advisors to check on the progress. Not wanting to be genuine and tell the truth (and be labeled a fool), each advisor plunges the situation into deeper darkness by fussing over the non-existent outfit.

Finally the day comes for the king to show his finery to the empire. The word has gone out to the subjects that this cloth is only visible to the "in" crowd. Everyone gets the message except for one little guy who can't read the memo. As the king is strutting through the streets of his dominion, this little genuine article blurts out rather loudly, "But he hasn't got anything on!" Little by little, a few snickers ripple through the crowd, then some outright guffaw. Soon there are people doubled over with laughter in the gutters. As if the scene were not bizarre enough, the last line of the story says, "This made the emperor anxious for he knew they were right. But the emperor thought, 'I must keep up appearances through the procession.' And the emperor walked on still more majestically, and his aides walked behind him and carried his imaginary train, which didn't exist at all."[4]

Fear and deceit ruled the community when the truth was submerged. Glee and relief took over when the truth surfaced.

You are a gift to others when you are real. You give a gift to others when you teach and encourage them to be real, as well.

'Tude. You are an immeasurable gift to others when you live godly attitudes yourself and then wisely instruct and encourage others to do the same. It is a source of constant wonder and relief to observe how markedly our lives can be changed, simply by altering our attitudes.

Your attitude itself is a gift to others. The manner in which you interact with them may touch them, encourage them, call them to accountability, or give them peace and refreshment when the going is tough. Your attitude can be a remarkable gift to others when you share it to such an extent that they pick it up and make it part of their own. As a bumper sticker says, "Attitude is contagious. Is yours worth catching?"

I have had three powerful role models show me the importance of making their attitude my attitude. Jesus of Nazareth, The Proverbial Woman and my Grandma Mary have all given me insights into passing on my attitude as a gift.

First, Jesus has graciously and plainly shown me the attitude of humility as described by St. Paul in Philippians 2:5–11:

> *Your attitude should be the same as that of Christ Jesus: Who, being in the very nature of God, did not consider equality with God something to be grasped, but made himself nothing, taking the very nature of a servant, being made in human likeness. And being found in appearance as a man he humbled himself and became*

obedient to death–even death on a cross! Therefore God
exalted him to the highest place and gave him the name
that is above every name, that at the name of Jesus ev-
ery knee should bow, in heaven and on earth and under
the earth, and every tongue confess that Jesus Christ is
Lord, to the glory of God the Father.

In our house, if you are uppity or high on your own stock, we say your are a bit too "full of yourself." Jesus was not full of himself in terms of thinking he was too good to do anything. He was extremely full of His essence when we realize that His very nature, His utter core, is loving service. He was so full of himself that he could empty himself of honor, aloofness, and power to show up on earth to represent the nature of God to those in desperate need of insight–us. When I'm feeling too good to make someone's sandwich or listen to someone's problem, when I don't have time to wipe a tear because I have something else to do, when I don't want to be bothered with petty, selfish and mean-spirited people, I am reminded of Jesus' example of attitude. I realize how blessed I am that He came to earth as my role model and guide. He provided food, listened to problems, comforted, sacrificed, and dealt with more ornery people than I'll ever meet! And His Spirit does the same for me each day of my walk with Him.

The second indispensable attitude is enthusiasm. If there is one word that describes the Proverbial Woman it is enthusiasm. She is described as strong, respected, generous, industrious, worry-free, and appropriately active. She rolls up her sleeves to dig into her day. She gathers, supports, encourages, and administers with energy and purpose.

Enthusiasm is the direct outgrowth of inspiration. Inspiration literally means we are working "in spirit." Lack of enthusiasm is brought on by several things. When we are overburdened by the details and minutia of life, when we don't really care about the project, when we are trying to fit a square peg into a round hole, or when we have said "yes" when we really meant "no," we are in danger of being despondent and frustrated by the tasks of life before us. When our vision is clouded by hurt, depression, or greed, enthusiasm cannot survive. True enthusiasm comes from walking hand-in-hand with God through the Holy Spirit who keeps us on the paths of peace and pleasantness. True enthusiasm is born of authenticity, of doing what we know we are called to do and not being tempted to take on other roles or tasks to please or impress others. A Proverbial Woman knows her mission, stays free of worldly attachments, and maintains divine connection with the guiding Spirit of God. Because of this she can pursue her life with passion, knowing the value of everything she does.

Lastly, there are few greater gifts we can pass on to the next generation than that of teaching and modeling gratitude.

My Grandma Mary was a sweet, simple peasant from the Ukraine. She literally "came over on the boat" and worked out a life with her husband, farming and raising eight children in Michigan. My father was her second son.

As is sometimes the case in families, we didn't see my father's side of the family very much, but I always knew my Grandma Mary was a woman of deep faith, truly devoted to God. One profoundly special visit from Grandma Mary came when my daughter Madison was about five, and my son Grant was one. I hadn't seen her in ten years, and my daughter had never met her at all. We decided to take Grandma to a concert one afternoon, so we all piled into our van, with Grandma Mary and Madison sitting in the second row.

The conversation between them was engaging and charming. Madison was fascinated with a story of a pink flannel nightgown Grandma had received the Christmas before. Grandma described its warmth and softness, and cooed over the fact that God had sent it to her at just the right time. She talked of how much she appreciated the gift, her warm and snugly treasure.

I sat at the steering wheel feeling like a total jerk. I was at the height of my selfish entitlement period and listening to her enthusiastic and genuine gratitude over a nightgown made my heart break for its hardness and melt for her authentic goodness.

Two weeks later, we received the phone call that she had died in her sleep. She died just as she had lived, quietly and completely resting in God's grace.

Madison and I made the five-hour trip to her tiny Michigan hometown for her funeral. On the way, we talked of Grandma's poverty, her many children, her pink flannel nightgown, and her love for God.

At the service, Madison asked for a few minutes alone at the open casket. I stood a respectful distance away, letting her have her space. I watched as her little lips formed a farewell to her great-grandmother. Then she blew a kiss and waved good-bye. As she stepped away, I moved in to meet her and asked her what she had said. Even at a young age, my wise daughter knew that some things are private. "That's not for me to talk about right now, Mommy."

On the way home, she said, "Mommy, do you want to know what I said to Grandma Mary?"

"Well, certainly honey, if you want to tell me."

"I told her she and I would always be friends, and I would miss her very much."

My grandmother had given my daughter a gift in just one meeting. She had touched Madison's heart with her own warm gratitude. And she had helped me on the road to recovery from the materialistic, possessive life-style by which I was being consumed.

Box up comparisons and put them on the shelf. They are not the packages God intends for you to open. They don't even enter the mind of the woman who is so busy being wise she has no time for self-defeating mischief. There has never been, is not now, and never will be, another one just like you. You *are* God's gift for others! If you long to build solid relationships with colleagues, friends, family members, and people in your community, you will make the greatest strides by embracing your unique giftedness in this world. Live joyfully in patterns, fabric, and music God has designed for you.

Your Proverbial Action Step

Reread the description in the first paragraph on page 28. Write the letters of our alphabet down the side of a sheet of paper. Creatively, humorously yet seriously construct a poem which describes your attitudes and characteristics. Savor your God-given essence. Embrace these attributes as your gifts to others.

God's Price is Right

Since 1956, contestants have been responding to the invitation to "Come on down!" issued by *The Price is Right,* one of the longest-running game show in television's history. Why is it so much fun to play and watch? Contestants love matching wits with the various games that promise big prizes if they make the right assessments about the value of various items. Viewers get a charge out of the sheer emotion displayed by players when they estimate correctly and win the prizes.

Max Lucado tells a story of two department store vandals who entered a store at night with great mischief on their minds. They didn't steal a thing, they simply switched the price tags on everything. If that wasn't bizarre enough, the next day the store opened for business and nobody even realized the prank for four hours. Lucado uses the story to make this point: we switch the price tags in God's world all the time.

In God's great game of *The Price is Right,* God's assessment of worth is always right. The Proverbial Woman is a woman who has placed her values in God's economy. She knows the inestimable importance of her mission and the rich returns of staying on her unique path. As she invests in wise speech, she reaps the benefits of spending her words judiciously. Knowing that the God of all abundance has graced her with all she has, out of gratitude she cares for and utilizes all of these gifts with energy and prudence. Because God places the highest value on His human creation, she keeps her life simply occupied in acts of service to all around her—any place and any time. As part of her stewardship and in special acts of service, she spends the gift of herself in lavish and loving ways on the people closest to her. Finally, she knows that God has placed supreme value on her as His beloved child. She keeps Him first and lets Him lead.

I hope you can see this woman portrayed in poetry as a springboard for looking at characteristics all of us can cultivate—no matter where we are in life. It is more about what we are than what we do. It is more about a life devoted to God, than a life wasted in comparisons, selfish ambition, and disorder. It has to do with everyday elements of our lives and using uncommon wisdom in a wild world.

Most of all, it has to do with the inescapable fact that you are deeply, passionately, and eternally loved by God. What He desires for you more than anything is a deeper, fuller, wider, and richer understanding of His gracious intentions toward and through you. My prayer is that as you comprehend this more thoroughly, and as your life is transformed, you will continue to accept Wisdom's invitation to walk and talk with her, learn from her, and change your world with her at your side. "Say to wisdom, 'You are my sister,' and call understanding your kinsman" (Prov. 7:3).

After all, the Proverbial Woman, the woman of wisdom after God's own heart, is you.

Endnotes

Chapter 1
1. Os Guinness, *The Call* (Nashville, TN: Word Publishing, 1998), p. 141.
2. Melissa Jansen, *Are You Kidding, God? Me, a Prudent Woman?* (Anderson, IN: Warner Press, 1998), p. iii.
3. Annie Chapman, "Why the Proverbs 31 Woman Drives Me Crazy," *Today's Christian Woman*, May/June, 1992, p. 63.

Chapter 2
1. Olivier Clement, *The Roots of Christian Mysticism* (Hyde Park, NY: New City Press, 1993), p. 17.
2. Cheri Fuller, *When Mothers Pray* (Sisters, OR: Multnomah Publishers, Inc., 1997), p. 30.
3. Fredrick Buechner, *Wishful Thinking: A Theological ABC* (New York: Harper & Row, Publishers, 1973), p. 95.
4. Anne Broyles, *Journaling: A Spiritual Journey* (Nashville, TN: Upper Room Books, 1999), p. 11.
5. Lord Chesterfield, cited in Robert Andrews, *The Concise Columbia Dictionary of Quotations* (New York: Columbia University Press, 1990), p. 300.

Chapter 3
1. Guinness, *The Call*, p. 175.

Chapter 4
1. Penelope J. Stokes, *Simple Words of Wisdom* (Nashville, TN: Thomas Nelson, Inc., 1998), p. 85.
2. Abraham Lincoln, as quoted in Bob Phillips, *Phillips' Book of Great Thoughts and Funny Sayings* (Wheaton, IL: Tyndale House Publishers, Inc., 1993), p. 228.

Chapter 5
1. Stokes, *Simple Words of Wisdom*, p. 109.
2. Mother Teresa, cited in Robert Serrou, *Teresa of Calcutta* (New York: McGraw-Hill, 1980), p.77.
3. Oliver Wendall Holmes, cited in Stokes, *Simple Words of Wisdom*, p. 108.

Chapter 6
1. Patsy Clairmont, "Not Her Again," *Focus on the Family*, September, 1999, p.3.

Chapter 7
1. Unknown author, cited in Laurie Beth Jones, *Jesus in Blue Jeans: A Practical Guide to Everyday Spirituality* (New York: Hyperion, 1997), p.282.
2. Fuller, *When Mothers Pray*, p. 33.
3. Henry David Thoreau, cited in Phillips, *Phillips' Book of Great Thoughts and Funny Sayings*, p. 317.
4. William King, *Hans Christian Andersen's Fairy Tales* (Philadelphia, PA: Running Press, 1996), p. 15.

Bibliography

Andrews, Robert. *The Concise Columbia Dictionary of Questions*. New York: Columbia University Press, 1990.

Broyles, Anne. *Journaling, A Spiritual Journey*. Nashville, TN: Upper Room Books, 1999.

Buechner, Fredrick. *Wishful Thinking: A Theological ABC*. New York: Harper & Row, Publishers, 1973.

Chapman, Annie. "Why the Proverbs 31 Woman Drives Me Crazy." *Today's Christian Woman* (May/June 1992): 62–63.

Clairmont, Patsy. "Not Her Again." *Focus on the Family* (September, 1999): 2–3.

Clement, Olivier. *The Roots of Christian Mysticism*. Hyde Park, NY: New City Press, 1993.

Clifford, Richard J. *The Wisdom Literature*. Nashville, TN: Abingdon Press, 1998.

Fuller, Cheri. *When Mothers Pray*. Sisters, OR: Multnomah Publishers, Inc., 1997.

Guinness, Os. *The Call*. Nashville, TN: Word Publishing, 1998.

Hybels, Bill. *Making Life Work*. Downers Grove, IL: InterVarsity Press, 1998.

Jansen, Melissa. *Are You Kidding, God? Me, a Prudent Woman?* Anderson, IN: Warner Press, 1998.

Jones, Laurie Beth. *Jesus in Blue Jeans.* New York: Hyperion, 1997.

—. *The Path.* New York: Hyperion, 1996.

King, William. *Hans Christian Andersen's Fairy Tales.* Philadelphia, PA: Running Press, 1996.

Lucado, Max. *No Wonder They Call Him the Savior.* Portland, OR: Multnomah Publishers, 1986.

Parrott, Les and Leslie. *Like a Kiss on the Lips.* Grand Rapids, MI: Zondervan Publishing House, 1997.

Peterson, Eugene. *The Message: The New Testament, Psalms and Proverbs.* Colorado Springs, CO: NavPress Publishing Group, 1993.

—. *Praying with Paul.* New York: HarperCollins Publishers, Inc., 1995.

Phillips, Bob. *Phillips' Book of Great Thoughts and Funny Sayings.* Wheaton, IL: Tyndale House Publishers, Inc., 1993.

Sailler, Ronald M., and David Wyrtzen. *The Practice of Wisdom: A Topical Guide to Proverbs.* Chicago, IL: Moody Press, 1992.

Serrou, Robert. *Teresa of Calcutta.* New York: McGraw-Hill, 1980.

Stokes, Penelope J. *Simple Words of Wisdom.* Nashville, TN: Thomas Nelson, Inc., 1998.

To order additional copies of

send $10.95 plus 3.95 shipping and handling to

Robin Chaddock
PO Box 353
Westfield, IN 46074

To contact Robin for speaking engagements:
Proverbial Women Ministries
317-842-0163
prowo31@dellmail.com